Richard J. Thain is Dean and Director of Placement at the University of Chicago Graduate School of Business. He has written two career-related books and has been a marketing professor and advertising agency executive.

THE MID-CAREER MANUAL

A Guide to Making
Smart Decisions
For Your High-Earning Years

RICHARD J. THAIN

A SPECTRUM BOOK

Prentice-Hall, Inc., Englewood Cliffs, N.J. 07632

Library of Congress Cataloging in Publication Data

Thain, Richard J.
   The mid-career manual.

   A Spectrum Book.
   Includes bibliographies and index.
   1. Vocational guidance.   2. Executives.   I. Title.
HF5381.T297   658.4′09   81-15430
                             AACR2

ISBN 0-13-581819-2

ISBN 0-13-581801-X {PBK.}

This Spectrum Book can be made available to businesses and organizations at a special discount when ordered in large quantities. For more information, contact: Prentice-Hall, Inc., General Publishing Division, Special Sales, Englewood Cliffs, N.J. 07632

10 9 8 7 6 5 4 3 2 1

Editorial/production supervison
and interior design by Alberta Boddy
Cover design by Jeannette Jacobs
Manufacturing buyer: Cathie Lenard

Prentice-Hall International, Inc., *London*
Prentice-Hall of Australia Pty. Limited, *Sydney*
Prentice-Hall of Canada, Ltd., *Toronto*
Prentice-Hall of India Private Limited, *New Delhi*
Prentice-Hall of Japan, Inc., *Tokyo*
Prentice-Hall of Southeast Asia Pte. Ltd., *Singapore*
Whitehall Books Limited, *Wellington, New Zealand*

Contents

Preface

For a self-centered set of creatures, human beings appear to devote comparatively little overt attention to their own careers. They may be relatively oblivious to the connection between occupational health and general health. Or, perhaps, what appears to be benign neglect is the same sort of code that causes males to display reluctance to look at themselves in a mirror within view of their friends. Their macho code seems to forbid this on the grounds that it reveals some form of conceit or insecurity. Therefore, they cast covert glances at themselves in shop windows or other reflective surfaces only so long as nobody else knows they are doing so.

Gradually, it has become more acceptable for men and women to talk about their own careers openly, following the trend toward more honesty and openness in all phases of our lives.

Openness has been fostered by placement and career counseling officials employed by the various types of collegiate institutions where it has become natural to discuss career problems openly. Students, alumni, prospective employers, and school officials have grown relatively more at ease and more expert in such matters. This has been a welcome change indeed.

I number myself among those who got involved early in helping career planners, both individuals helping others and individuals working on their own behalf. The task has been to bring some semblance of orderly perspective to an inevitably individualistic process without forcing the necessary creativity and originality out of it.

In the last decade there has been more literature on the general subject. However, it has contained very little planning literature and an excessive amount of crash material designed for the executive who finds himself in need of a crash program for getting a new job. Such "crash" activity is sporadic and frenetic at best, often a cookbook of quick and superficial schemes that may represent a route to career satisfaction but that are more likely to lack the thoughtful substance of which lasting management careers are made.

A career is a story. Except for the very oldest in body or in spirit, it is a story unfolding. To keep it from unraveling, one needs to be able to lay it out on a spool, frame by frame, for self-editing. The idea is to develop one's own ability for self-criticism and introspection. Every healthy person should feel a sense of personal drama about his or her own career.

A Hebridean Gaelic proverb has it that God created mankind because God was fond of stories, and that the rewards have been suitable because the majority of mankind are pretty fair weavers of tales out of the fabric of their own lives or of those about them.

We would maintain that such a tale or case is the place to start. Even as a psychoanalyst prefaces his career by being psychoanalyzed, so a serious careerist is wise to assess his own story.

The closer the individual can come to accurately and selectively setting forth his or her own story and understanding the implications and promises of that story, the closer to the realization of its potential will the tale come.

Working as a career counselor for students and alumni in early and mid-career ranges, I have determined that the latter have fewer people supporting them. The mid-careerist is working alone and blind, whereas students at many schools are being served by placement office staff and support. It is to provide support and guidance to the often bewildered mid-careerist that this work is undertaken.

I have derived support from the multifarious college and alumni placement officials, employer recruiters, alumni, students, friends, and the many people who serve as anonymous, but nonetheless real, case examples in these pages.

The most specific thanks are extended to the Graduate School of Business of the University of Chicago and its dean, Richard R. Rosett, for freeing some time for this work; to B. J. Amina Johnson, for her skilled role as editorial assistant; and to my wife, Jane, for her patience and support, as always.

CHAPTER ONE

Early Mid-Career

Two personal events took place in Chicago and New York, respectively, on March 24, of one recent year. In Chicago, the setting was a convention called the Women's Career Conference. To it, Alice Palmer, along with hundreds of her sisters, made a pilgrimage dedicated to kindling or redirecting career hopes. She attended specialized sessions and interviewed companies and schools at display booths they had rented. She roasted inside her managerial wool suit in the crowd-generated heat and the excitement of it all.

How nice to feel courted, to feel wanted! Alice paused to buy a soft drink in a corner of the grandiose hall. As she sipped her drink, she recalled the televised injunctions of a Black leader, the Rev. Jesse Jackson, to his followers. Over and over he had reminded them: "You are somebody!" Alice was fired up by the repeated exhortations to the women that she had heard that day, and was inspired to say to herself, "By God, maybe I am somebody!".

Her final stop at the show was to drop into a seminar at which a panel of representatives of five local universities were embroidering on the theme of why a woman should undertake work toward a graduate business degree. To the relief of the standing-room-only crowd, the school people finally completed their harangues and opened the meeting to questions.

Alice raised her hand and asked, "Can a high school counselor get a good business job if she takes an M.B.A.?"

"That depends on the age of the counselor," came back the answer from the only female panelist, and the males nodded assent. "If she is over thirty, it may be difficult. It is hard to change horses in mid-career."

Alice said no more, being one who never came close to divulging her age. As she walked toward the parking lot a few minutes later, she drew up her coat collar. The chill was not altogether a product of the weather.

Later, eating dinner with her husband, she asked, "George, am I old?"

Her husband smiled, laid down his fork, and said, "Hell, no, 'cause if you are, honey, I'm even older."

"George, are you and I in mid-career?" Her husband doodled with his fork on the paper doily and took his time answering.

"Well, yes, now that you mention it, we're at least in early mid-career. Not the same as being middle-aged though." He frowned a little, as he returned to stabbing the TV dinner.

Too Young or Too Old

Nicholas Gregory was seated at one of those modern window walls looking a bit nervously down beyond his foot at the Manhattan traffic many floors below. Such windows always bothered him, and job hunting always bothered him too, and there he was, talking to an executive search consultant, a "headhunter," about switching jobs.

"And so," Nick was saying, "I've come to you to see if you can help me find a better job."

"Nothing I'd like better," chuckled the other man. "That's my business. But I'm afraid you're here a couple of years too early. My clients are looking for people thirty-five and up and making their age, as they say, $35,000 or more. You're thirty-two and making only $26,000 you tell me. I seldom get orders from my clients for people in your bracket. No offense, but you just fall between the chairs. Too old to start from scratch, too young to be moved in upstairs."

Such shocks of recognition are delivered every day and everywhere. For a good many people, in what we might call the second stage of working life, the words of the once popular tune hit home, "They're either too young or too old."

These second-stage or early mid-career people find themselves part of a population segment that is growing fast in absolute and comparative terms. Their large numbers are partially responsible for the phenomenon referred to as the "graying of the work force." They are in "the bulge," the products of the post–World War II baby boom. They have been powered and equipped for business and the professions by the fervor for education that has propelled increasing numbers of Americans through collegiate institutions.

Parameters of Early Mid-Career

What are the parameters of early mid-career for people in management-oriented jobs? The boundaries are certainly not exact. Along the dimension of experience, early mid-career begins after the period of training, orientation, or apprenticeship is past. Whatever the official length of the training period, this early gearing up will last from two to six years. These are the years in which most managerial aspirants and some technical people, such as engineers, are said not to earn their keep but to be subsidized by their employers.

Since most people prepping for management are college educated, for them the first stage will not be surmounted before age twenty-six. For those who go on to graduate school or return to school after a hiatus for work, early mid-career may not begin until later than that. So the early mid-career era definitely cannot be delimited by strict age parameters. For many, it is complicated at the same time it is enriched by the urge for continuing formal education. The U.S. Department of Health, Education and Welfare comes up with the amazing figure of twenty-eight as the average age of collegiate enrollees. Night schools are aglow, as are other forms of part-time schooling at all levels. Women are moving out of family activity or lower-level jobs. Determining the work stage on a basis of age alone is thus not valid.

Yet, such determination will be practiced by employers unless they are reminded by their employees of some of the exceptions such as those noted above. And it has to be admitted that in the majority of cases early mid-career will commence in the later twenties and earlier thirties.

It is wise for people who are at the more extreme ends of the spectrum, close to the ages of twenty-five and forty, to stress that, despite what may appear to be chronological discrepancies, they cannot be thought of as too young or too old because of their early or late starts. Some of the older people may have to join the work force at entry level. Some younger people may already have a foot in the top managerial suite by age thirty.

There's an ancient Scottish folk song celebrating a cross-eyed cook who kept "one eye on the pot and the other up the chimney." A mid-career person has to keep one eye on his or her personal career stage and the other on chronological age. Keeping the balance can be as delicate as cooking a soufflé.

We live in an age-conscious society in which we tend to type people by their presumed ages before other judgmental evidence is in. Employers proceed in a similar fashion. Before they were prohibited from doing so by law, they were accustomed to listing in their "help wanted" advertisements such specifications as "wanted: controller in mid-thirties; salesman, between 35 and 40." The major dividers lay and still lie in the numbers 30, 40, 50, and the multiples of five in between.

People who have passed 30, 35, or 40 can vouch for the power of these figures in our culture. This is a chronological variant of slot-mindedness, justified or not, and a chimney on which one must keep an eye whilst stirring the career pot.

Slot Mindedness

Slot-mindedness refers to the tendency on the part of employers to hire or move people ahead in deference to relatively set tracks. If a person is an accountant by second career stage, it is hard for employers to think of him or her as anything else in the future.

Also, employers have a way of matching the specific job held against the age of the individual. If one person makes senior analyst by twenty-eight and another by forty in the same company, the younger person is usually held to be more worthy of promotion. This is the civilian equivalent of a military personnel phenomenon known as "age in grade." A person who is "overage in grade," too ripe for the rank held, is often regarded as unworthy of promotion and therefore a prime target for early retirement.

Someone working in private business or government or nonprofit administration has got to reckon with multiple factors in impressing employers with his or her worthiness of promotion. Among them are:

1. Past performance
2. Future promise and flexibility
3. Current compensation (in relation to age, grade, and future pay)
4. Career Stage

We are certain that point four, career stage, is taken into account by most employers, but still only muddily understood by them. In planning and negotiating advancement, it can be particularly important to those in early mid-career to recognize their own career stages for purposes of self-assessment. It is important for them to be able to translate this assessment to their senior colleagues in order to explain why they may be ahead, on time, or behind schedule in the minds of these bosses. Any of these three conditions can be put forward as reasons for advancement, but each of them can require explanation.

No other career tier is filled with such a variety of stair and chair levels as early mid-career. First-stage people have in common that they are all beginners. By later mid-career the die tends to have been cast and the mold is set.

We are talking about a crucial period into which one appears to move in all too swiftly and out again as fast. It is an age in which physical and mental vigor can be strong enough to sublimate natural anxieties and doubts and lead to that kind of occupational fruition that has got to be one of the highest incentives to a well-examined life.

CHAPTER TWO

A Professional Managerial Stance

Recruiters for business and industry will invariably list "professionalism" among their leading criteria for hiring management people. They seldom define this quality, and what they mean by professionalism will vary from person to person. When they will commit a definition, it probably will include a sense of perspective of and pride in the managerial role. Personal and professional integrity is implicit.

It is highly possible for an early mid-career person to have been working at a job for some years and to have made no effort to see beyond that job, to develop a philosophy about his or her craft that stands up to positive evaluation by people monitoring that individual's progress and quality.

For a mid-career person with little or no managerial experience, it can be even harder to develop an occupational attitude that can be termed "professional." Let's examine the role of the professional manager.

Whether you are already a manager or an aspirant to that role, you sense that it isn't as finite a profession as law or medicine. Those ancient professions have their parameters defined by academic requirements and professional licensing examinations.

With the exception of the profession of public accounting, business careers are not of such limited access although, of course, the development of business schools and the advantages of such degrees as the M.B.A. indicate a narrowed access to certain areas of work.

The breadth of products, services, and institutions to be administered in the world is staggering. The people charged with running the entire panoply of human enterprises can be called managers. They keep government, schools, businesses, industries, museums, orchestras, armies, villages—the whole world of human institutions—running. Could there be a more important set of callings?

The individual job of the manager, executive, administrator, or whatever you choose to term it is many faceted. It is clear that the modern manager has inherited a mantle from the kings, generals, chiefs, tribunes, and statesmen of history. From the top on down, certain leadership traits are expected. American political rhetoric is filled with allusions to that ability to lead, to inspire, and to rally that seems a natural concomitant of the responsible jobs.

There is a school of managerial social psychology that sees leaders and managers as two different types of people. The leader, they aver, is a daring, charismatic, and imaginative risk taker. The manager is a conservator, manipulator, and compromiser who tends to be preoccupied with smoothing the present rather than with thrusting toward the future.

While we are quite able to catch the implications of this line of thought, the fact remains that a profession of leadership has not been developed. An administrator who displays leadership is still a manager, director, or vice-president on his calling card, and not listed as a leader.

The ultimate kudos appear to go to those who can manage other people at the same time they lead them, with a proper mix of flamboyance and caution. Such people are in short supply. If you are one of them, and can find ways of bringing these talents to light, your future is assured.

So, leadership can be part of it. A very big part is the patience and skill required to draw the best out of subordinates and to get people from disparate disciplines working together effectively, even without direct control over them. Such performance can match excess responsibility against lack of direct power. It is the ultimate test of good managerial traits.

For these reasons, management is often described as an art, calling for qualities that may be honed but that are hard to instill and to teach if the basic talent is missing.

Management is often referred to as a science as well. As a science, it is being researched and taught in business schools. A body of knowledge has grown up, blending findings in economics, psychology, and the other social sciences with the qualitative disciplines and real world observations. This blend of theory and practice renders much more legitimate the claim that management is on the way to becoming a truly professional discipline.

While granting that the average manager can scarcely claim to be a social scientist, many of his professors and some of his researchers can make this claim.

It takes no great stretch of the imagination to view the manager as a species of social science applicator, just as one may envision an engineer as an applicator of science without, strictly speaking, being a scientist.

It has taken time for historical recognition of the legitimacy of management as an entirely respectable set of professions worthy of the best of talent. Plato and the ancient Greeks regarded as inferior such callings as philosophy, war, and agriculture. Canon law and the various guild strictures during the middle ages tended to class people in commerce as second-class citizens whose semiusurious existences were tolerated out of necessity and who were taxed sorely by the landed aristocrats and military adventurers.

Gradually, with the opening up of international marine trade culminating in the political and industrial revolutions, the commercial classes came into every semblance of power and into some semblance of respectability.

Even in the United States, the most business-based society the world has known, there are still a number of families who would prefer that their sons and daughters not "go into trade," as it were. In many other modern countries, the social estate of the businessman is lower than in the United States.

Antibusiness feeling was strengthened during the tumultuous late sixties and early seventies when many student-aged Americans regarded businessmen as dangerous, war-mongering pariahs.

However, during the seventies, the enrollment of many of our best youth in business schools and economics courses has been phenomenal. This has been due, in part, to the growth of a more individualistic and practical attitude among young people.

These changes have coincided with the drying up of opportunities in academics, science, education, and law, while the business job market remained fairly stable and viable.

One may view managerial professionalism in quite another sense too. Apart from the matter of degrees, certificates, and schooling, one can adopt the athletic view of a profession.

A professional athlete is someone who invests his life in his sport. He is not only more proficient than most amateurs; he takes his sport very seriously. The professional manager displays a similar commitment.

One can argue quite persuasively that American business is results oriented. It would be foolish to deny that the strongest criterion for success is a proven record of contribution in the past to employing enterprises. For some types of work, such a record would be enough whether the manager had a thought at all about the history, philosophy, or sociology of the managerial professions.

However, a person whose accomplishments at mid-career include evidence of hard-nosed results, plus well-articulated respect for business as a profession, is likely to go further in the subtle higher reaches of general management.

Perhaps you have already sensed, when observing higher executives, certain statesmanlike qualities. Not that they are all renaissance giants, but there is a tendency to find them more thoughtful and more professional than the commonality of business executives.

How does one improve this professionality and add depth and perspective to his or her stance? Intellectual curiosity, fed by reading and attendance at lectures and seminars, and education, of course, formal and informal,—these are the ways. There is further comment on the importance of education to advancement later in this book.

CHAPTER THREE

Career Options

Someone who has gone only so far as to opt for a career in management will not find this a narrow decision. The variety of such jobs is enormous, so enormous as to be baffling. Being an accountant, a steel salesman, or a hospital administrator may seem to lack common threads to someone who does not study the jobs closely. This can result in considerable frustration in selecting directions in early career.

If one hews to the theory that many careers are attempts at articulation of youthful dreams, the dream of being a businessman, executive, or administrator is probably less well formed than that of being a doctor, lawyer, writer, or policeman. Management has ever represented a widely variegated lot of skills.

What are the options open to satisfaction seekers in the administrative arts and sciences? It is probably necessary, or at least helpful, to create a model to render the alternatives more graspable. Some comment can be superimposed upon the model structure to suggest the personal traits most appropriate to each field.

Why a model for people already a way into their careers? The answer is that very often experienced people are more limited in their views than students. Schools tend, at least, to survey the world. Many people, once on the job, put on blinders that limit their vistas to their own desks. Later on, when exposed to further education, many find new perspectives are the principal benefits they have derived. They catch visions in executive programs, for example, of alternatives they never new existed. Some of these fleeting goals are not reasonably attainable. For ambitious and intelligent people, the striving can be more important than the attainment.

Schools of business have reasonably standard ways of setting up curriculum that can help in the classifications for our model. Here is a way of laying out the functional or specialty areas of business.

Marketing

Marketing is a broad blanket under which a host of occupations are more or less handily stuffed. They are all concerned with extending, moving, or selling products and services. Marketing is variously described by its practitioners as "the shooting end of the gun" and as the sector where profits are made. Sales is obviously "on the firing line." If products and services cannot be moved (sold), all the bricks, buildings, accountants, and machine operators mean nothing.

Mixed with a species of line arrogance, marketers often display an inferiority complex. It is a carryover of the "trade can be vulgar" syndrome that is felt strongly in marketing. Breathes there a mother who rapturously boasts about "my son, the salesman"?

Sales

The cornerstone of marketing is sales. In many ways it is the great training ground for people in the whole marketing area. How better can you come to know the product and its market than through selling?

Most of the jobs that interest people of managerial potential call for the sale of industrial goods or services—one factor or business selling to another. Often the applications of these products are complex and require fair brains to understand.

Selling of this sort is a species of consultancy. The salesperson must know the customer's business well enough to propose solutions to special problems. Often, a salesperson is presenting a whole new system of doing business, not a single piece of hardware. A good example of this is the business machine salesman who is selling a whole new way of keeping records and, incidentally, is selling or renting appropriate machines.

Sales Management

The sales force produces those who reach sales management, one of the staple routes to line preferment in companies. Generally speaking, these jobs are best for sturdy extroverts, although people with less than forward traits have made studiously impressive salespersons for complex products.

Retail Buying

Retail buying is the center fold of retail store activity. It can lead to store management, although the management and buying functions in retailing are often quite separate. Retailing partakes of aspects of show business and thus can be a satisfying career for people with a feel for style and display.

Advertising

Advertising may be aptly described as marketing communications. With its print, video, radio, and direct mail aspects, it draws a wide spectrum of talent from among writers, design artists, photographers, cinematographers, directors, and musicians. Here is a chance for the artistically inclined to gain satisfaction through identification with a definite art form. Advertising can be called "the liberal arts of business" and, as such, has a wide appeal as a work site.

Some advertising workers are directly employed in the advertising departments of the companies doing the advertising. Many others, particularly in the consumer goods field, work at advertising agencies in the mainstream activity of creating the ads for their clients. The agencies have a tendency to be the principal locations of advertising talent.

The sale of advertising space and time occupies a certain number of "business side" advertising people as opposed to those on the "creative side."

On the business side of the spectrum also lie the agency account executives and marketing people, those professionals who interpret the agency's work to the clients. Here, an understanding of the business roots of advertising overshadows the artistic endeavors.

A set of occupations providing a similar link between the client and the agency is that of brand management. These people are charged with directing the total promotional effort for given brands of packaged consumer items. As such, they interface with agency account people and often trade places with them in the course of job exchanges.

It should be remarked that many times jobs in the areas so described are relatively scarce—with the exception of sales jobs. Selling posts are almost always available—on salary, commission, and mixed arrangement. Selling talent is in tight supply, whatever the economic climate.

The old axiom, "He who controls accounts is never out of a job," applies year after year. Selling remains the easiest path for interfunctional job changes. It is a particularly good avenue in which a product knowledgeable and technically trained person can ease over to the management side of the spectrum.

Physical Distribution

Physical distribution of goods, including transportation, storage, and warehousing, obviously develops myriads of jobs that, although often overlooked by marketing inclined people, are truly at the heart of such pursuits.

Production

Sharing honors with marketing as central line functions are the various jobs that revolve around factory and machine production. Generally calling for technical undergirding of some sort, such jobs involve command and control over people and machines or, on the staff side, the furnishing of data to those who control production. So many collegians have in recent years shied away from such work that this has opened considerable opportunity to their fellows who are willing to "get their hands dirty."

Computer-Related Jobs

Allied to these "hard" production jobs are the various computer-related operational jobs that help both service and manufacturing businesses to dispatch the thousands of paper transactions that are essential to their existence.

Various computer-oriented jobs require programmers, managers, and researchers to mediate between machine and men. Here, once again, one finds many openings because of the disinclination of college graduates toward roles that seem dead-endedly technical. To take such a view is to misunderstand the workings of modern business. So essential to the conduct and profitability are these jobs that managers so trained are being brought into top ranks. The margin of profit in a large commercial bank, for example, tends to be made or missed in the way it handles its complex set of operations.

Various operations researchers and internal consultants are applying the techniques of mathematics, statistics, and the computer to the weave of corporate and institutional life.

Finance

These people can likewise be regarded as financial analysts, since they are trained on the financial health of the companies.

At the soul of the organizations are the financial planners, looking toward future disbursement of money—the financial lifeblood.

Allied with them in the financial panoply are the treasury people, who are charged with the allocation of a company's monetary holdings. They are dealing with investments, bank deposits, and disposition of cash and securities.

While the planners and the internal consultants are looking to the future, the contemporary fiscal health of a company or institution and a record of its historical health are guarded by the accountants.

On the company side, accountants are known as controllers or comptrollers, generally subordinate to the chief financial officer.

Their auxiliaries outside the business are the public accountants certified as to their skills by passing Certified Public Accounting examinations and winning the coveted C.P.A. designation.

The C.P.A. firms perform a training and indoctrination role for many of the people engaged in corporate accounting. The crossover from accounting firms to industry is a heavily-traveled bridge of value to all parties concerned.

External auxiliaries to the corporations and institutions extend beyond the public accountants to include the commercial banks, insurance companies, investment banks, and management consulting firms.

Corporate entities in their own right, the commercial banks and similar financial institutions offer advice on money and various business systems. A common figure in that world is the commercial lending officer who evaluates credit risks, at the same time filling the liaison role between the banks and their customers.

The investment banks are underwriting support for corporations through marketing their stocks and bonds to the outside world through institutional and retail salesmen after these offerings have been developed by corporate finance specialists.

Management Consultants

General management consultants exist to offer auxiliary service in each of the functional areas, providing both a third-party view and a species of expertise that the average corporation or institution is not likely to possess within its own staff.

Personnel

With the people, the most important factors in most institutions, it falls to the personnel or human resource people (as they are coming to be known) to conduct the hiring, firing, training, development, and the evaluation of workers and managers. A fair part of the mediation between society's rules (as reflected by government regulations) and the employers is carried on by the people in this area.

Personnel jobs have, until recent years, been regarded as wise to avoid by many of the more ambitious professionals.

The idea, not unfounded, prevailed that most companies paid lip service to the importance of personnel, but by and large relegated it to people with very little power or prestige within the organization.

Happily, this sort of disuse appears to be vanishing, as more importance is attached to these areas of endeavor and their representatives move up closer to the godhead in organizational hierarchies.

Opportunities seem better on the human side than ever before, particularly for people with social skills, engaging personalities, and an ability to counsel their fellows. Needless to say, backgrounds in the behavioral sciences and experience in education are pluses for this sort of work.

General Administration

General administration is akin to the human resource category. Such people manage offices and their physical as well as human problems.

General administration is often confused with general management, but should not be. In the most commonly accepted business lexicon, general management consists of the higher officials of a company whose duties transcend specialty and include overall responsibility for several functional areas. It is usually necessary to move into such a category before becoming a top official of a company.

All these functional options exist not only in private industry but also in government jobs and posts with such institutions as universities, museums, and orchestras. Whatever the auspices, the principles are the same. One can often pass from one sector to the other.

Self-Exercise

Career Options

The various components of the functional model are laid out below. Rate these areas (1, 2, 3, 4, etc.) which appeal to you. If your current position does not seem to be leading to one of your top choices, this is a signal for attempted change.

Functional Model	
FIELD	FILL IN YOUR RANKING
Marketing	
Sales	

Functional Model

FIELD	FILL IN YOUR RANKING
Advertising	
Physical distribution	
Production	
Computer-related jobs	
Finance	
Consulting	
Personnel	
General Administration	

Suggested Readings

FIGLER, HOWARD E. *Path: A Career Workbook for Liberal Arts Students.* Cranston, R.I.: Carroll Press, 1979. Integrated sequence of exercises for assessing work-related values.

LEVINSON, DANIEL J. *The Seasons of a Man's Life.* New York: Alfred A. Knopf, Inc., 1978.

MILLER, ARTHUR, and MATTSON, RALPH. *The Truth About You.* Old Tappan, N.J.: Roselle Park Press, 1979. The importance of key motivators and how to detect them.

MINTMEIR, C. DOUGLAS. *The Employment Game–Where Do You Fit?* Pittsburg, Pa.: Carnegie-Mellon University, 1977. Helpful perspective.

TERKEL, STUDS. *Working.* New York: Pantheon Books, Inc., 1974. Often depressing but realistic set of interviews with people at work. Does provide ideas for interim jobs that can afford access to permanent opportunities.

THAIN, RICHARD J. *The Managers.* Bethlehem, Pa.: College Placement Council, Inc., 1978. Essentially a prose model of the options presented by the world of administration.

CHAPTER FOUR

Educational Background, Foreground, and Future

A good education has come to be regarded as a central element in success. When we speak of someone as educated, we may be commenting on that person's possession of general knowledge, technical information, social poise, or a combination of these qualities. The graces of education tend to be inobtrusive when they are present, but when they are lacking they can be most obtrusive.

With the general rise in the formal education level, the majority of people of professional or business promise have by early mid-career acquired the general minimum acceptance level of at least a B.A. or B.S. degree.

There are still some equivalents of the "mustang" which is, in the military parlance, someone who has worked his or her way up through the ranks without much college education. Mustangs in business life are growing rarer.

To carry the military analogy further, our managerial and administrative society tends to be double tiered, after the fashion of an army. There are officers and there are enlisted people. The former increasingly tend to be college graduates, the latter to be noncollegians. These distinctions, rather than birthrights, form our social class base.

It is significant that the term "officer and gentleman" is applied to those men on the degreed side. This is a further reflection on the identification of education with social skill.

17

One need only witness a labor negotiation to be able to note attitudinal differences between college-educated management and noncollegiate labor that go beyond the cosmetics of dress.

Degrees of Relevance

If there is a standard university degree for professional management and administration, it is the Master of Business Administration (M.B.A.) degree or its equivalents, the Master of Public Administration (M.P.A.), Master of Science in Industrial Administration (M.S.I.A.) and some related species.

These are generally programs of two academic years of full-time study or part-time variants that take a longer time to complete. The mention of part-time programs points up the fact that the early mid-career person who feels a need for education can usually find a way to make it up on a part-time basis at almost any level.

Any individual who lacks the initials at the bachelor level is well served to proceed on a part-time basis to make up that lack. This is true even when the person heads his or her own enterprise and is not concerned with bolstering the personnel file. A degree can add both a polish and an additional assurance that can stand such people in good stead.

Broad undergraduate education offers a heightened world grasp plus a honing of skills in figuring, writing, and speaking. Undergraduate or graduate management or economics schooling provides further perspective on the world of affairs, the mechanics behind that world, the language and jargon of that world, and an acquaintance both with immediately useful technique and cutting edge theory applicable to the future.

An Educational Inventory

Those at any mid-career stage still have need to assess what elements are lacking in their educations. Some come equipped with solid B.A. or B.S. and M.B.A. backgrounds. Chances are that further formal classroom work would be superfluous.

Some may lack much of any schooling. Still others have law or other advanced degrees in fields more extraneous to the professions of management. For them, formal schooling in management could be an aid to their own understanding as well as a beneficial exhibit with which to bolster progress at work.

When lawyers, scientists, engineers, or academics switch to becoming administrators in their own degreed fields, they do enter a set of occupations that ask for the exercise of a different set of muscles and that require adjustments of attitudes and competencies. Managing people and budgets becomes the heart of work, rather than activity in the laboratory, the classroom, or the court. Continuing education for their new roles is often indicated.

In Search of Change Agents

Continuing education can, of course, take many forms. It may or may not lead to a degree. Universities, consulting firms, and employers field a number of educational courses, seminars, and workshops to benefit people of a wide spectrum of backgrounds. Such programs can help cure stagnancy in a world where, as George P. Kelly, President of Marshall Field and Company, puts it, "You have to change even faster than you grow." The relevance of the education is important, so that selectivity is quite necessary. Someone a fair way into a career does not have an unlimited amount of time in which to play schoolboy. We have perhaps all come to have far too much faith in the power of education to change us substantially, too much faith in the power of degrees.

Degree Potency Erodes

Certain it is that the degrees held by a manager recede in importance as the career progresses. From time to time school credentials may pop up to an advantage as personnel files are being combed for particular kinds of backgrounds, but achievement gradually becomes more important than old diplomas.

The fresh credential, the newly-acquired degree, or nondegree educational experience carries some impact when acquired in early mid-career. It may signal that old George, the engineer, is bidding to be new George, the manager; that Mary, the one-time secretary, can be considered in line to become a corporate officer.

However, a person who adds a new degree in part-time schooling cannot expect instant promotion or recognition for it. Many bosses will maintain that he or she remains the same person as before. They will point out that degrees have little magic to endow the timid with courage, the dull-witted with intelligence, or the socially maladroit with charm.

Education of any kind interferes with time on the job. Such a trade-off has to be measured. Not every employer is overjoyed that one of his people is enrolled in an outside course. He may begrudge the time, and he fears the consequences. Latter day scholars have a tendency to push for promotion or to quit and go elsewhere when they complete their programs.

It is well for the mid-careerist to gauge the trade-offs between additional study and the job.

As in so much related to career, self-assessment, added to what external advice is forthcoming, is essential. Further education and training is not good as is.

Criteria for Enrolling in Educational Programs

Those contemplating additional education should ask themselves:

1. Do I honestly have a need for the program's purported content? (Granting that it is hard to know in advance of what a program will consist.)

2. What is the program's reputation? What is the reputation of the sponsoring organization? Have I talked to enough people who have been through it?

3. Does my employer endorse it? Could it increase my chances of advancing my career where I am or elsewhere?

4. Do I have time for it, given the demands of office, travel, family, and personal life?

If the answers come out negatively on any of these scores, it is wise to turn the "opportunity" down.

For a younger person with fresh credentials, the degree is vital. It is chiefly what the employer has to go on. Nondegree programs of shorter duration make increasing sense with the passage of the years. A new degree from a prestigious full-time graduate business school carries with it a maximal institutional halo effect. It is a ticket to an interview program richly studded with employers eager to buy, and it offers a "fish in the barrel" opportunity for the graduate to interview many more employers than he could possibly cover as an individual.

Returning to school for a prestigious program at the M.B.A. level can be a worthwhile investment for an early mid-career person who by the late twenties has little to show but some tepid or irrelevant experience. Beware, however, that during every year after thirty it becomes more difficult for a newly-degreed person to establish believability with employers if previous job experience has been inappropriate. Society has a subconscious way of restraining experienced persons who seek to make widely swinging changes of direction in early mid-career.

Some disillusioned Americans have come to regard themselves as overeducated. These include the plethora of advanced degree holders in fields in which there are no jobs. For such a person, an added degree—even an M.B.A.—may generate negative employer reactions. "What is this guy, a career scholar who has never held a real job in his life?" To stop short of another degree could be wise in such a case. A lot of education can be a dangerous thing—if it seems to have been inappropriately focused.

When an early mid-career person is urged or ordered to take some schooling by his employer, it will usually be at the expense of that employer, often with some time released for study. This becomes a difficult mandate to refuse. Whether such a program is for a day, a week, or many months, it can usually be taken as an augury that somebody has promotional plans for the individual asked to attend. Occasionally, such opportunity is merely a gesture to substitute for the impossibility of tendering a promotion and a raise, but such sops are not common.

Whether or not a course of study is endorsed by the employing organization, it can be used as promotional leverage. Often one needs to attract attention either within the present employment context or with a new employer. A new degree or course completion adds some evidence of change, new excitement to a career, and tends to make a change seem more logical. Completion of a course, attendance at an extended symposium, a new degree—all these qualify as achievements, creating plausible reasons to ask for advancement or for a new job.

Bosses or employers are given to asking, "And why have you chosen this particular moment to push for a change?" One logical answer: "I have just completed an M.B.A. program at night. In it I learned some things that I would like to apply to my work, but they are not as applicable on my current job as I would like them to be. I've learned some new concepts, caught some new visions, and feel that I have new knowledge of advantage to you."

Those attempting to induce promotion by use of the educational lever have a tendency in our mobile society to think in terms of having to change employers. This is not necessarily the best way to go, since progress with one's current employer can save some of the inevitable wear and tear involved in a change of scene.

Trying first "back at the ranch" is logical before "kicking the tires" in the general market. One needs to transmit restless eagerness for improvement to current bosses. It can be helpful to have them aware that they are bidding against outside competitors. Such a game of nerves requires a sense of confidence and security that not everyone possesses.

An early mid-career person who picks up such degrees part-time as the M.B.A. or a master's degree in engineering can usually expect some help in placement from the degree-granting school. This will be provided on a confidential and individualistic basis, rather than in the open hiring hall atmosphere of the full-time programs. Chances of making a new connection through the part-time school placement office are slimmer than those for full-time students.

All of this is not to say that additional education should be sought for raw advancement purposes alone. A fundamental criterion for such undertakings can be the satisfaction of doing both a more efficient and a more understanding job.

Personal enrichment unrelated to a job is always a worthwhile educational motive. As careers coalesce and shape, as aspirations level off in response to the realities that the top of any organizational pyramid is very thin, the dimensions of personal growth over and beyond the job can become increasingly important.

Early mid-career people often wrestle with the idea of adding a night law degree to their holdings. Unless they go directly into the law, such study is more on the enrichment score than it is directly applicable to management. It has to be granted, though, that the increasing social involvement and social complexity of a litigious society makes sophistication in the law a personal asset and, in some instances, a bolstering factor in a management career.

Advanced degrees in such technical fields as engineering may strengthen administrative progression in a highly technical business. Chances are, however, that additional management education is a far better bet for a leg up the managerial ladder.

There are various dimensions that business schooling can add to mid-career strategy. First, it can provide a broad overview of the setting of business, its history, its romance, and its vistas. Tom Bullenger is a case in point. Here, in his own words, is his description of the state in which he found himself:

I, Tom Bullenger, was a child of the early seventies. In college, I loathed business and what it stood for. Together with my classmates I regarded capitalism as a reactionary force responsible for the Vietnamese war and attendant evils. But I couldn't earn a living picketing firms making war materials and singing protest songs, so I "copped out" and eventually I took a job with a paper cup manufacturer as a sales trainee.

Well, it's hard to be a salesman without enthusiasm, but that was me all right. Somehow I stood the paper cups and calling on hamburger franchising companies hawking supplies for their stands or stores. I began to appreciate the thrill of new business sales, kinda like fishing, but I sort of hated myself for starting to enjoy it. I still had no real respect for my job. I remember that when the minister of our church used to pop off at our men's club about how venal business men are, I said nary a word in our defense.

Trouble is I knew nothing about economics or business beyond my little cups, and had nothing to say. I was an American Lit major in college and I remember spending hours puzzling about all the ambiguities our prof said Moby Dick stood for to Captain Ahab. Business was my white whale—a giant creature I didn't understand, yet here I was chasing him.

I described this to my manager, Charlie Flint, one time. He's a pretty bright old bird and he nudged me into taking a course in economics at a local evening school. I enjoyed it more than Melville, took another, then another. Read Adam Smith and David Riccardo and then came up to date with a course which pitted Kenneth Galbraith against Milton Friedman. Somehow business and economics all came alive for me. I began to enjoy my job because I could appreciate what I was up to. The white whale seemed to shrink in size.

Got to where I was pretty good at answering the minister back. Matter of fact, I had the guts to remind him the other day that the way he makes his living—by his mouth—selling ideas he called it—isn't far from my way, and ideas often hold less water than my cups.

The Technician Turns

Nobody needs education more than a technical person trying to become identified as a manager. It's tough enough for graduate engineers to make the switch, but it was even tougher for Morris Cooper, who was not a college graduate.

Morris was a Black American who got a laboring job right out of high school in a big steel mill. He talked his way into permanent day shift with a sympathetic foreman, carried on his education at night in a community college, and wound up with a technician's two-year certificate in metallurgy and a foreman's post by the age of twenty-six.

Morris liked school, did well in it, and managed to get into a good M.B.A. program by dint of a fine performance in CLEP, a college equivalency test that, in rare instances at rare schools, enables a person to overcome the handicap of being degreeless and still get into graduate school.

Vision of Finance

In the M.B.A. program, Morris caught a vision of finance as his occupational goal. He became increasingly adept at financial theory and midway in the program tried to switch jobs from the outlying steel mill to the company's downtown home office as a financial analyst. Morris was a good technician and his bosses at the company blocked the move for many months because they didn't want to lose him at the mill.

Finally, Morris was awarded the M.B.A. degree and made his heavy bid to cross from technical operations into financial management. He consulted both the placement director of his school and the personnel manager of his company. The three of them got together and hatched a plot. The placement director helped Morris go into the job market. He garnered three bids from other companies to become a financial analyst. The personnel director helped Morris present these bids to his bosses. The opposition melted and a post at headquarters in finance was forthcoming. Education and a "bit of three-way cahoots" turned the trick, as Morris put it.

Education and Career Strategy

In the case of the paper cup salesman, further education served as an internal strategy to change a man's attitude toward his work and its place in the world.

In the situation of the steel company technician turned finance practitioner, the subject learned some financial skills at the same time he was taking on an external identification that enabled him to present a new professional face to the world. Knowledge and credentials are both important. Formal education can be a route to both.

Pole for Vaulting

Early mid-career represents a time for a vault to more generalized responsibilities for specialists if indeed they are to make that leap. Most managers and administrators begin with some sort of specialty, so this is a period in which they may need education for the new role almost as badly as in the younger traditional school years.

We have the scientist who becomes director of research, the physician who turns to directing a hospital or a clinic, the professor who becomes a dean, the school teacher who becomes a principal, the business analyst or staff person who assumes a line or command role. New muscles, new techniques, and new perspectives are called for. Some of these changes evolve naturally enough, others need to be induced or strengthened through some type of formal or informal education.

Professor Turned Dean

Let's take a case of a professor turned dean. This is his own testimony:

> I was named dean of our liberal arts school at age thirty-five after a few years of teaching history. I was considered successful in the eyes of the world, but after the initial glow of achievement with each promotion, I could see myself in a less radiant light. I was bedeviled by schizophrenic pulls after I was voted in as dean. I had done my work writing and teaching in the renaissance period, with a natural emphasis on Italy. I knew very little else.

> I tried for awhile keeping one foot in Florence, journeying back both physically and spiritually. But I had too little time, and my scholarship became watered wine compared to my previous standards. I could not keep up with the new readings, let alone turn out many contributions of my own.

> I had to keep substantial office hours. Every time I turned around, there was a complaining student petitioning me, a faculty member wishing to discuss tenure or more money, or a committee meeting which I had to attend.

> I recall one time coming across an exciting ancient volume near Livorno, buying it, and bringing it home. I had just begun to lay it out in my study to dissect deliciously when the phone rang. It was the president of the university querying me as to how our fund drive was coming.

I was galvanized into action by guilt, and it was weeks before I ever picked up my precious volume again.

Fortunately, the dean of our business school had become a good friend of mine. When I admitted to him that I felt myself a rotten dean and a watered down professor, he undertook to recommend a reading list of volumes to cure my deficiencies on the deanly side.

I read a book on the marketing of nonprofit enterprises. It gave me some ideas for fund raising. Two accounting texts, one budget text, and a finance book bolstered my interest and competence in budgeting.

The best book was one which drove home the idea that administration is a profession and that by George if I was going to be any kind of a dean, my life of the mind would have to play second fiddle to running things and coping with money, budgets, salaries, and people.

I came to realize that far from being regarded as intrusive into my garden of academic delights, people were my business as an administrator. Now I think I'm beginning to earn my salt in my new role.

Don't Forget Self-Education

This professor turned dean interview could have been conducted with any of the myriad other specialists who elect to become or are forced to become generalist managers by early mid-career. Formal education in business or administration can be helpful, but the self-taught or reading list approach can be significant for others who cannot take the time.

Not everyone has a friendly business school dean as a collaborator, but nearly everyone has a university bookstore within fair reach these days. Go into the store, browse among the titles, and look at those assigned to classes listed in the school catalogue that seem relevant to your cause.

Nobody will award you a diploma for this kind of self-advancement, but it can certainly take the bafflement out of those mid-career problems where education holds a key.

Self-Exercise

Should I Enroll?

If contemplating taking on an educational program, your answers to the following questions should *all* be "yes." If not, devote your time to your current job and personal life.

QUESTIONS	FILL IN YOUR ANSWER
Do I honestly have a need for the program's content?	

QUESTIONS	FILL IN YOUR ANSWER
Is the program's reputation strong?	
Does my employer endorse it? Can it advance my career here or elsewhere?	
Do I have time for it, given the demands of career and personal life?	

Suggested Reading

EPPEN, GARRY, D.; METCALFE, DENNIS B.; and WALTERS, MARJORIE E., *The MBA Degree*. Chicago: Chicago Review Press, 1979.

CHAPTER FIVE

Variant Employer Styles

One of the more encouraging observations one can make about American business is its pluralism, the fact that seldom are two companies alike in the way they are organized or in the way younger executives are developed.

In some sense this may inhibit some standardization and job interchange, but where it is great is that what a disenchanted person at one place can do is simply transfer to another company with quite a different philosophy. It can be a refreshment to switch at the same time it makes equivalent posts harder to gauge.

It can be desirable for talented early mid-career people to attach their fortunes to companies with a clearly defined fast track. Such companies take certain categories of promising graduates (that is, engineers or M.B.A.'s) and set them on a clearly demarcated line of ascent. If you are one of the chosen ones, this company is for you. If you do not make that track or fall from it, chances are you will want to turn elsewhere where you can feel like a first-class citizen. Where the demarcations are eminently clear, it is valuable for people either on or off the preferred list. It solves the "limbo" problem of not knowing where you stand. It removes, one way or the other, the uncertainty that plagues so many mid-careerists unable to get a straight answer as to how they are doing.

One common type of company could be called the sink or swim. New hires are thrown into the pool of real work with little preparation. If they are resourceful and lucky, they swim; otherwise, they drown. The wastefulness of such a procedure is manifest where, with a little guidance, some of the sinkers could have been saved. Those who survive such immersion are always inordinately proud that they did, and perpetuate the method or nonmethod. Like jet plane test pilots, they have proved they have macho doses of "the right stuff."

At the other end of the spectrum are the very cautious companies that train for one, two, or three years. Commercial banks are almost always in this mode. Lending officer hopefuls attend formal classes within the bank for between six months and six years.

Just as sudden immersion can be spooky, so long class exposure can be exceedingly tiresome to young people who are heartily tired of schooling.

The optimum may be a mixture of some formal class-like training along with assignment to real jobs.

It is anathema to mid-careerists switching from one firm to another to have to submit to some type of training. Orientation, perhaps; training, no. Sometimes, of course, it is merely a matter of nomenclature.

It is certainly wise for an early mid-careerist evaluating companies to investigate matters of organizational style. He or she may find, for example, that both at the bottom entry levels and part way up entry as well, the company in question may have an internal consultancy management. The new hire is dubbed an "internal consultant" or perhaps a "planner," both tricky terms in that their meanings vary so from company to company. After working at what is essentially an internal trouble shooting role, applying analytical solutions to multifarious functions, the company decides where the new hire should be placed. Such a process may last for two or three years, and hopefully the trainee has some say in his or her placement.

Take the matter of Johann Wohlgemuth, a young Swiss graduate of a top M.B.A. school. He expressed himself as bewildered but nonetheless titillated by his early experiences.

During the opening months, Johann was assigned to an internal audit task force that was poking its collective nose into the bookkeeping business of every segment of the company in turn. This provided him a broad view of the entire company.

He next found himself engaged in putting together a new incentive package for a field sales force that previously had operated solely on a salary basis.

Then he was assigned to determining whether or not his company should go into the business of manufacturing pea picking and canning machines. The basis of his approach was to assess the market for canned and frozen vegetables.

His eventual permanent assignment lay in the vegetable machinery area in which he had a strong hand in development. Needless to say, he felt that kind of proprietary interest that is such an important ingredient in holding early mid-careerists on the job.

One type of organization about which an early mid-career person can and should be wary is the one with a very flat table of organization where titles are vague, and given out sparingly.

When people with such companies try to translate over into other companies, they can find no equivalent jobs. Their titles do not carry weight.

I recently tried to help a good man make a jump from a manufacturing company where his title was "assistant to the manager of planning." For this he was paid $70,000. However, we wouldn't get $70,000 worth of believability here. The title, which in some companies would have been vice-presidential, was not heavy enough to transmit the weight.

CHAPTER SIX

Diary of
a Fast Tracker

By this time in this book, the value of laying out a flexible career plan, with course corrections to adjust to events, should be obvious. We will examine alternative modes for such steering. Managers still are given less to planning for themselves than for bulkier abstractions such as corporations, governments, and societies.

For many people, the Career Diary or log, a running set of periodic entries, establishes the chronology that can be reviewed against periodic plans. Such a record should provide a running analysis of career progression right after events happen. A thorough approach involves keeping the diary alongside the Career Plan and graphing a Career Excitement, Salary, and Promotion Chart so constructed that career health can be projected out of the totality at any given point.

We have been made privy to both the Career Diary entries and the thought processes of Kevin Nolan, a person who feels that his own planning and tracking systems have been so helpful that he agreed to share them under an assumed name to cover his identity.

Kevin's initial timetable looked like this:

College: B.A., Economics (R.O.T.C. Commission), to age 22

Army: 3 years, duty as quartermaster, to age 25

Business School: 2 years M.B.A. program; majors: Finance and Marketing, to age 27

Manufacturing Corporation: 2 years in Financial Analysis, to age 29

Management Consulting: 4 years and then to corporation as planner, to age 33

Corporate Long-Range Planner: 2 years, to age 35

Corporate Division General Manager: 3 years, to age 38

Group Vice-President: 3 years, to age 41

President and Chief Operating Officer: 3 years, to age 44

Chairman and Chief Executive Officer: until 50, thence to politics or public career

Kevin had begun his Career Diary of what actually happened three months after graduating from an M.B.A. program in June, Year 1. The diary read:

Things are going well. I certainly can do the financial analytic work with Sheppard Corp. The boss seems well taken with my expertise at matching expenditures by product line and factory location against plan. He says he's going to take me with him when he makes his year-end presentation to the chief financial officer so I can explain the details. Don't know whether to believe him or not. Selfridge and Allen warn that he's a brain picker who may well leave my work unacknowledged.

January, Year 1—Ashley (the boss) did let me make a presentation before the old man (Trudd, the financial chief executive). Could tell I made a hit. The old man asked me where I learned the regression technique. I told him from Professor Armons. He indicated he'd heard Armons give a symposium on energy costs and had been much impressed.

March, Year 1—Promoted today to chief financial analyst and now youngest chief in the department. Boss tells me I'm on a really fast track. Scares me a little, but it's good to be here. Means $2,000 more a year. Sallie is overjoyed. Now if I can skirt my boss and get working directly for financial "veep," it'll be great.

June, Year 1—Today I received notice I go to work as long-range planner for Mr. Trudd, the financial chief. I'm already a couple of steps ahead of Ferguson and Latta, who graduated with me and are still plain financial analysts. More money, new office, and a chance to work under Trudd. I'll have to watch my step. They say he's tough.

September, Year 2—Trudd is proving great to work for. I'm going to sit at his elbow during his meeting with the investment committee of the board of directors next month concerning proposed merger with Beauvoir. Good Break!

December, Year 2—Beauvoir merger fell through. Trudd's got me working now with investment bankers on possible amalgamation with

American Brace. I'm afraid I'll do work and they'll get credit. Well, anyway, I'm working closely with our directors on the deal. Checking against my career plan the other day, by now, I thought I'd be a management consultant. Can't leave now, however, too much excitement here and I'd hate to ditch Trudd.

March, Year 2—Hot diggity! Trudd called me in this morning. He seemed a little sad and I thought somehow I'd goofed on American Brace. Before I could ask, he says: "The chairman tells me he's had his eye on you. Wanted me to probe on whether you'd be interested in becoming secretary to the board." I've learned enough to control myself, so calmly asked Trudd how he'd like to lose me. He said he wouldn't but that these are the breaks and he left the move up to me. I grabbed the chance. It means $70 grand a year and that'll put Sallie and me in fat city. I can't afford to cross over into consulting now.

June, Year 2—It's great working for the chairman. He told me to call him "Al" the other day. It made me uncomfortable, but if that's what he wants, that's what he'll get.

September, Year 3—Learned today that chairman will take early retirement first of year. Since I'm his creature as board secretary, I wonder where that leaves me. Sallie teases me that I'm too young to retire. Rumor has it that Trudd may become president (I hope) and current president could become chairman.

December, Year 3—Black day, I think. Schmidt has been brought in from American Brace as chairman, president remains where he is at; Trudd stays put as financial veep. What becomes of me?

January, Year 3—Today I got the answer from Schmidt. Wants me to stay on as secretary of board. He was vague, however, when I asked where I would go from there and said we'd have to wait and see.

March, Year 3—Today Jeremy Tell, C.E.O. of General Microfiche, called and said he wanted to talk to me. He was on the board of this company for a while as an inside director and at one point chairman of its finance committee before he took the General Microfiche job. We always got on well.

April, Year 3—Well, I'm going to go with Tell and maybe straight to hell. I'm getting nowhere as secretary to the board. Tell offers $90,000 per year as assistant to him for two years and then, more importantly, promises a crack at the line, probably as a division general manager. Sounds too good to pass up. Sallie doesn't mind moving to St. Louis because we have good friends there. Well, here we go!

September, Year 4—I'll be glad when my "assistant to" term is up. I'm a bit more of a personal lackey to one man than I was as secretary of the board. I've talked my new chief (Tell) into two months' worth of detached service in general management at the St. Louis plant to fill in while the manager is away at a special school.

December, Year 4—The general management stint at St. Louis was exciting. I'm definitely for that. Running a show by myself intrigues me.

At least when the boss isn't around and I get to do some of the work in place of the parent, so to speak.

May, Year 4—No more talk about a line assignment. The boss is off on a kick that we've been spending too much money on outside management consultants. He's probably right. Wants to build an internal consulting cadre and hints that someone with a background such as mine should head it. I'm wary.

September, Year 5—"You're so good at staff work, how'd you like to be named internal planning chief?" Those words cut into me today as I shared an in-office lunch with Tell. I told him I was flattered, but I'd get more enjoyment out of running something. "Ever thought of sales?" asked the chief. I said I had thought of sales management. The chief said I needed some kind of seasoning for general management and he could arrange it for me at no depreciation in salary. This lack of a raise shook me, but I found I was feeling a bit stagnant and a look back at my career chart sold me on the idea.

November, Year 5—Well, here I am in charge of microfilm and microfiche sales for the company in the state of Missouri. The big sales I participate in myself, like the one the other day to the state government general services administration. Each of my 12 salesmen seems fairly competent. I'm beating around the state a bit too much for my taste, but Sallie doesn't seem to mind.

February, Year 5—My state sales team exceeded quota by more than any other region in the first half of this year. I'm doing something very right. Most of all, I've learned I can lead and inspire and sell all at once. Funny, I never really saw myself as having much to do with sales.

June, Year 5—Back on bright news trail with assignment as marketing manager for all states west of the Mississippi. Tell took me aside for a whole day together with Lemmery, the national marketing veep. Tell stressed the importance of the new role. He and Lemmery both say they expect great things from me.

November, Year 6—Lemmery doesn't seem too friendly any more. I don't know what I've done, except perhaps done too well. My assistant, Max Josten, overheard Lemmery mutter something about "that damn fast track M.B.A." Sounds like I pose a threat. I don't see too much of the C.E.O. of late either. Maybe Lemmery's slipping some misinformation to him. I'd better watch my step.

January, Year 6—The other shoe has dropped. Lemmery has, in effect, told me to be prepared to clean out my locker in the next few weeks. He claims I'm not performing as expected. The chairman is soon to retire. I don't really know the president. The company will cover my tracks with other employers, but where to turn?

March, Year 6—My friend, Kim Jacobs, was right. The headhunters were the places to turn. Scott and Bliss came up with a marketing v.p. job for $90,000. Weeks and Mayo produced a smaller company executive vice-president slot with promise of becoming chief operating officer in a few months. Merriweather, our outplacement counsel, unearthed a division vice-president and general manager slot with Colossal, a really big company. I'm putting my money on that one. No promises, but they're desperately short on young talent. They're offering $120,000 per. I think I have a shot at the presidency in three years and I'm definitely still on the fastest of tracks.

It'll give me control over some manufacturing too and that's what I need to round out the picture.

Never did get in that management consulting stint, but for me it would probably have been just a way stop anyhow.

Now's the time to review the original Career Plan against the Career Diary and plot an Excitement, Salary, and Promotion Chart (see opposite page). This work follows:

Self-Exercise

Future Timetable

Here is a planning framework for the future. Filling it out and checking it for possible modification annually will keep your goal focused. Start at your current age. You may set the age brackets as you choose, but the following schedule is a fairly typical sequence for a fast track:

PERIOD	FILL IN YOUR PLANNED ROLE
Age 25 to 27	
27 to 29	
29 to 33	
33 to 35	
35 to 38	
38 to 41	
41 to 48	
48 to 60	

Self-Exercise

Tracking Projects

Construct a timetable for yourself along the lines of Kevin's, shown at the start of this chapter.

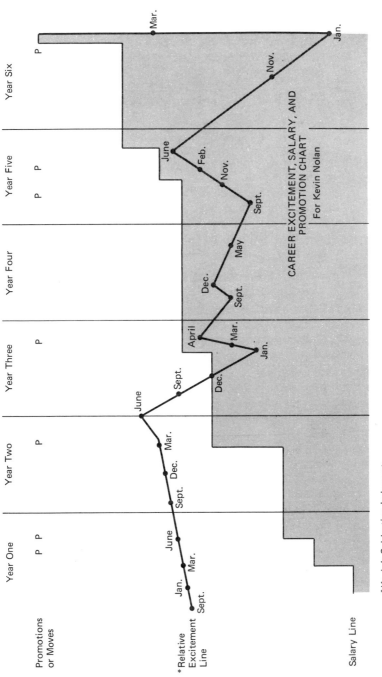

CAREER EXCITEMENT, SALARY, AND
PROMOTION CHART
For Kevin Nolan

Promotions
or Moves

Year One   Year Two   Year Three   Year Four   Year Five   Year Six

P   P   P   P   P   P   P

*Relative
Excitement
Line

Sept.   Jan.   Mar.   June   Sept.   Dec.   Mar.   June   Sept.   Dec.   Jan.   Mar.   April   Sept.   Dec.   May   Sept.   Nov.   Feb.   June   Nov.   Jan.   Mar.

Salary Line

* Kevin's Subjective Judgment

Consider keeping a Career Diary henceforward in which you note simply those dates when significant events or conversations occurred that bear on your career.

Such milestones occurred for Kevin every few months. If they are not popping up with some regularity in your life, you should take some steps, as he did, to induce them—to attract attention and consideration.

CHAPTER SEVEN

Sustaining Momentum

Kevin's plans and chartings reported in the previous chapter record a brief span of the work life of a successful person. While it is comparatively rare to be making over $100,000 per year in the sixth year out of school, it *is* being accomplished by some. A mid-stage manager on a more modest track needs, even more than a fast tracker, to resort to devices akin to Kevin's to chart his crises of confidence, peaks, valleys, and logical take-off points.

Is There a Dynamic?

It is vital to be able to determine whether a career has sustained enough of an internal dynamic to overcome dangers of flagging long before later mid-career when upward mobility is more likely to slow because of the paucity of opportunities in the upper organizational reaches.

By taking his own excitement temperature at various stages in his diary, and laying it out against his salary, Kevin acknowledges the necessity of trying to inject periodic doses of the adrenalin of accomplishment into his career. He does not buy any more than we do that intense physiological wear-out can be expected before the sixth decade of life, while admitting that energy varies with the person.

Nor is Kevin's path stoneless. He is forced out of one job near the close of his chartings. Clearly, his bosses have had a tendency to think of him as more of a staff person than a command person. You could tell even from the arm's length tone of his diary that he was puzzled and hurt by this reaction, but he didn't confine his reaction to being puzzled and hurt. He deliberately sought temporary general management experience in the St. Louis plant, a courageous act that took him off the track for a time, so that he could prove himself to himself and others.

Sales as a Rite of Passage

Likewise, he knew some sales experience was for his own good, and he took a modest sales management job with no increase in pay as a necessary rite of passage.

He had the fortitude to shy away from internal consulting, although it was pressed upon him by the chief executive at one point.

In short, Kevin did not drift. He sought to remain in control of his direction. The sustained motif of his plan was to become a line executive and then a chief executive officer. Near the end of his chronicle to date, we see him coming into general management responsibility. We do not doubt for one minute that such a determined person will reach his goal.

Sustaining momentum toward career fruition consists of establishing a goal, making certain the stimulation never goes out of the chase, making quick and firm decisions at strategic moments, having the fortitude to turn down moves that will deflect from the main course, and sensing empathy both with various co-workers and bosses—the skilled use of people, if you will.

A Realistic Attitude

Kevin sensed early on that he was *non grata* to Mr. Lemmery, and that he never would be popular with him. He did not agonize much about it; nor did he seek to psychoanalyze the other man. He understood that while a manager is dealing with social science, he is not necessarily a social scientist. He needs to know what the human climate is without necessarily understanding all the systems behind the weather, painfully aware that meteorologists are only a bit less baffled than laymen.

One can be an economic interpreter without being an economist, an effective human resources practitioner without being a psychologist, or Machiavellian in the straightforward, rather than any kind of sinister, sense.

It is clear to see that Kevin is adept at sustaining visibility, which is a necessity for one who would sustain momentum. He is able to find jobs that expose his ideas to important people. He starts out finding ways to present his ideas to the financial chief, soon to the directors and the chief executive officer. Without a constant search for such exposure, any good person may be wasting his fragrance on the desert air. An artist is presumably less fulfilled without an audience. Good works that go unknown may vent the soul, but they do not advance more corporeal causes.

A very hard concept to get across to students and other species of idealists is that, although doing good work is important to success, if the right people do not know the work has been performed by you, the accomplishment may have a hard time emerging with your tag upon it.

The Meek Inherit Nothing

Without being a sycophant, Kevin early on is performing before the right people. He has been lucky, sure, but he has also cultivated an important managerial knack of sustaining momentum by sustaining visibility. We have observed a generation of business school graduates making their way. There is one sentence we whisper to them as we pat them reassuringly and send them off into the arena, and that is: "Get to know as many vital people as you can." Whether it's a summer job or a "permanent" one, it is well to eat few lunches alone. Get to know your bosses, your associates, and your customers. They do not necessarily have to be big shots, but they should be folks who are bearers of information, education, perspective, pleasure, or a combination of these values.

Even discounting for the fair weather variety, if one has enough friends and acquaintances (and, of course, a record of some accomplishment), one need seldom feel stymied in career progress. Recall that Kevin, in his last recorded stanza, was tipped off by friends to use some executive search firms, thus enlarging what might be described as his information pool.

The Search Network

Reputable executive search firms can be somewhat official and commercial friends, in need or not. They are, in effect, opportunity brokers, and can be of great help at various junctures in a career. Once they get to know you and your abilities, they may call you at any time they represent a firm with an opening. Many times they are not after you, but any recommendations that might occur to you as to an appropriate person to fill an open assignment from a client. Sometimes they are after you, but more often they covet your ideas about someone else. No matter, sooner or later they may have a job you feel you can't turn down, but, of course, the good thing is that you have the option of turning something down.

One mark of success for any manager is the degree to which the executive search firms seek him or her out. A number of referrals can't help but reflect the fact that you are unusually able and successful.

Some Misconceptions About Search

Failure to sustain career momentum can result from failure to interpret and evaluate internal satisfactions. It can result from complacency, or lack of daring, in responding to outside stimuli. One might posit that any person will pay some attention to a job exploration that may be of great benefit, but we have not necessarily found that to be true. Part of this can be laid to the fear or mistrust of the search man, the "headhunter." Actually, many of the search firms are most reputable, and have a great deal to offer a targeted individual.

We have been party to some highly conscientious searches in which great care was exhibited to match the parties well when the client would actually have settled for something less scrupulously perfect.

Some search firms may be more desperate for business than their rivals, and there are, no doubt, charlatans in the field. Certain employment agencies may well deserve the "body shop" appellation foisted on them. However, most so-called third-party firms in the recruiting field are serving an economic function, or they wouldn't exist.

Despite the fact that search firms are chiefly useful for people who already have good jobs, some of them will provide gratis advice to friends seeking changes.

Aid Sparse at Younger Edges

The trouble with all of these true search entities is that their aid is seldom available to younger and lower paid mid-careerists. They tend to confine themselves to jobs falling in the over $30,000 per year category because they are generally compensated by a commission percentage of the first year salary paid by the new employer. Even when they are funded by hourly billing or some other compensation plan, the prestige of the firm rides on the level of the jobs. When they have a lesser job, they will often apologize with "Please understand we very seldom conduct a search at this low a level. We are doing it merely to accommodate a valued regular customer."

The gist is that many early mid-career people have, as we pointed out in the first chapter of this book, little access to the major search firms and more dependence on employment agencies. They also can tie in with the employment counselors, those firms who will counsel job applicants for a fee. The counseling firms purport to help with counseling, testing, resume writing, and circulation of resumes. If they help much with any of these for a couple of thousand dollars, they may be accounted unusual. We have found but a sprinkling of helpful individuals in firms of this category.

Outplacement Firms

A relatively new variant in the job counseling firmament is the so-called outplacement firm. It is retained by substantial employers to help people they fire to new jobs. As an act of good will and conscience, such entities can prove quite helpful to everyone concerned.

To echo a previous chapter on education, the greatest external job search assurance one can have offered in the $20,000 to $30,000 yearly salary category is to be allied with a good school placement office. Whether to current student or alumnus, these services are usually free.

In sustaining proper momentum, an early mid-career person needs all the complementary help he or she can get. Search firms, alumni offices, professional associations, newspaper ads—wherever one can register—so much the better. It's like an advertisement: the more exposures it can have to broader publics, the more certain it is of being effective.

Where Do I Stand?

The most difficult phase of a career strategy is self-assessment. First, it's the obvious difficulty of evaluating your own talent against that of others.

Then comes the matter of evaluating your progress against that of others who are moving ahead or falling behind you. Such gauging probably will be based on title, on salary, and on imperfect information (shaded with rumor). People who are doing well generally know it, and are not loath to share such information as salaries with their fellows. We find on cross-checking surveys that it is the least successful respondents who fudge on the truth.

Ask About Numbers

Ask search people and alumni placement people about salaries. "How am I doing?" They'll pull some fairly accurate numbers out for you. They'll have a feel for them just from working with such figures day after day. Former classmates and alumni groups are likewise good sources of information and support.

There are a certain number of more specific surveys, such as those carried out by the Association of M.B.A. Executives, listing salary averages of M.B.A. graduates from some of the leading M.B.A. schools. Individual placement offices generate some similar figures yearly.

Business and professional associations can be the best places in the world from which to derive statistics that may help to advance one's job cause.

A Search for the Numbers

Pavel was quality control manager for a garment manufacturer. There weren't a large number of such people in the country. In trying to negotiate for progress within his own firm, he felt isolated and without anything beyond what would sound like artificial caprice to go on.

By chance, at one large garment convention he met two other quality control managers. They exchanged some information on techniques and decided to organize a small meeting of their fellows the next year. The following year they met again. There were about ten others at a quality control session this time. When they turned to salaries, they anonymously handed in their respective numbers to a common pot and disclosed the range of salaries without disclosing individual figures to their employers. Pavel was shocked to discover that his salary was the lowest of the lot. Needless to say, at the next salary review he brought out the figures. His boss was shocked too, and produced a decent raise that brought him more closely up to quality control standards.

He had discovered also that his job description was too meager, and obtained some redress of that set of definitions as well.

In short, in the act of sustaining momentum, one must have some sort of fix on how fast he or she is traveling in relation to others. Likewise, some exhibits from the world universe of other similar organizations are helpful. When you appear before some constituted tribunal seeking alteration of status and salary, it's well to be armed with some pertinent figures for the discussion.

There have been some old rules of thumb about salaries that have been rendered obsolete by inflation and the passage of years. One such was that a manager should be making his or her age in thousands of dollars: namely, $30,000 at 30; $40,000 at 40. To fall much below these figures would be low, but there are components to success other than money.

That seems a rather odd statement to have to make, but after some time of dealing with Americans and comparing their values to younger Europeans and Asians, we have to come to the conclusion that when values are expressed in terms other than cash, Americans place comparatively little value on them. One frequently hears the comment, "I don't care what I do, what my title is, or what my honors are, so long as they pay me well."

People from other countries, including those behind the Iron Curtain, value other kinds of perquisites, such as official automobiles, vacations abroad, summer homes, access to goods, club affiliations, office size and location, insurance, and travel. These kinds of perquisites are most often honored in economies short on consumer goods. However much money you make, there is just so much you can buy, so they seek access to intangibles that money won't buy.

Affections Other Than Money

It is well for the American assessing long-term desires and his shorter-term fever charts to ruminate upon less inflationary objectives, as well as money. It is our observation that, with mounting taxes and mounting personal age, nonmonetary perquisites take on increasing importance. Such movement has been exacerbated by energy shortfalls that emphasize such benefits as easy commutes to work.

Squeaky Time Down South

We used to have a southern colleague (until he became too successful to share our office) who had marked on his wall calendar, at various intervals, the words "Squeaky Time." When asked what this meant, he would sing, "When It's Squeaky Time Down South," paraphrasing a once-popular tune, "When It's Sleepy Time Down South."

As the weeks rolled closer to his dated reminder, he would request a date with our boss to squeak, sometimes squawk, about his career. With our rather self-absorbed boss, and that's a fairly common malaise, you had to find ways of attracting the boss's attention to problems beyond himself in order to remind him that you and your problems *did* exist.

Inducing Labor

It is the unusual employee who does not need to petition for some squeaky time in which he can corner his superior or superiors for career discussions. In long-established theory, managers are to regard the bringing along of subordinates to succeed them as part of their higher obligations. In practice, the employee frequently has to initiate the procedure. When you stop and think of it, the subordinate has an obligation, too, to let his employer know what his plans are and where he would like to go. Complete certainty or candor may be unattainable or inadvisable, but it certainly helps for both parties to have hoisted some signals in advance of events and decisions. Bosses may not always approve the suggestions, but they will generally cock an appreciative ear to evidences of planning of any nature.

In presenting a case for advancement, the approach trick is to propose moves that will benefit your listener and the organization, and not just the proposer alone.

Get the "Me" Out of It

Never say: "I think it's time for me to advance my career by being promoted to"; rather, say: "I've reached a point where I think I could advance the company (department or section) by turning my attention more fully to a sector that's been ailing for some time." Never say: "Frankly, I'd like your job, Mr. Wilkie." Laudably ambitious as this may seem, this threatens all but a very unusual superior.

Better to say: "I'm trying to pattern myself after you, Mr. Wilkie." That kind of almost spiritual succession sounds gentle, and Mr. Wilkie will be subconsciously relieved by a vision of somebody trying to recapitulate the master mold.

Entrepreneurial Momentum

So far, we have been focusing on the momentum of the individual within the larger organization. For the small business participant, or especially for the small owner-operator, the problems can be so very different that we reserve that discussion for a later chapter.

Self-Exercise

Career Excitement, Salary, and Promotion Graphing

For a graphic and comprehensive overall picture of your career to date upon which to plot the future, you may wish to try your hand at the six-year Career Excitement Chart opposite. A filled-in example of this chart appears on page 35.

The lines may reveal to you that you are truly in the doldrums or perhaps that you are doing unusually well.

Suggested Reading

BROSEMAN, EDWARD. *Confronting Non-Promotability; How to Manage a Stalled Career.* New York: AMACOM, 1977. A hard look at the classic problem.

	Year One	Year Two	Year Three	Year Four	Year Five	Year Six
Fill in a ''P'' where you have been promoted						
Fill in peaks and valleys of excitement						
Fill in a salary line						

CHAPTER EIGHT

The Critical Autobiography

Over the past twenty years, we have consistently heard from graduate business students that among their most valuable courses is one that forces them to lay out a plan for the rest of their careers. This plan is inevitably coupled with a critical autobiography in which the subject lays out for his or her own eyes, and perhaps for others' eyes as well, the candid history of the career to date.

Such a history is never completely objective it is true, but it is an essential act nonetheless, and it will probably be more valuable and more accurately representative of that life than any other document.

In some ways, such an exercise is a confession. It begs for an objective look, since one has a hard time fooling oneself altogether, and there is no value to such deception.

Perhaps the Critical Autobiography is based on a philosophy similar to that which dictates to the psychoanalyst that he be psychoanalyzed himself before beginning practice.

Purely in the interest of providing an illustration of what we're talking about, the author here submits to the reader his own autobiographical thought processes. These can likewise be submitted to a third-party voluntary adviser who can function as a biographer if he wishes, but at the very least as a third-party referee. Such exposure is a recommended process in putting a critical autobiography to the best uses in advancing a career.

The Autobiography Begins

My earliest serious job lust, beyond the common youthful policeman/ fireman imaginings, was to become some sort of a writer. As nearly as I could tell, this desire seized me partly because my teachers had identified me as a fair writer. By the time I was fifteen, I was the editor of the high school literary magazine, *Soft Pipes,* and the published author of a few thin and precious poems and essays often contrived to assure my English teachers that I was receiving from them some valuable coaching. It seemed but a matter of time and schooling before recognition would bloom beyond the range of my prim faculty adviser's desk.

Progress was a bit slower than I had anticipated, and a variety of youthful diversions deflected my more serious aims for a few years. But my faith did not waiver that I would have the reserve power to be a WRITER when cornered into earning a living.

Left to the Extracurricular

My collegiate career went well enough, and in order to hold up the honor of my family and my fraternity in what were known as extracurricular activities, I began some desultory writing for college newspapers and magazines. The future looked freer from controls and less rigorous than if my choice had turned toward heavy investment in legal studies or a more formal professional career. "Comfort and freedom" was my motto. Mental and physical laziness were unacknowledged but were undoubtedly very real considerations. As for money, it was not much of a factor until my later collegiate years when I fell in love and needed money to marry and when military service socialized what had really been a tranquil life with nurturing parents and a fine young woman to shield me from hard career decisions.

No complaints. Disturbances like wars and growing up are harder on many people than they were on me. I dropped out of college for my last year, seeking some stable work before World War II military service. The line of work that seemed realizable would be allied with writing.

Some distant relatives of mine were very bright people who were editors and publishers of a weekly insurance magazine—trade journals, we called them in those days. I spent an instructive year as a reporter and a junior editor.

The job seemed pedestrian to someone who still thought of journalism as something more Runyanesque than reports of automobile insurance rate increases. As a consequence, when a new morning newspaper was founded in Chicago a couple of months before Pearl Harbor, I joined the staff as a cub reporter.

A Crackling News Season

That was an exciting few months, as news crackled all around. Draft physical standards changed, I was drafted into the Army Air Force and, after a few weeks of training as a radio operator, I managed to talk my way into the military occupational specialty of editing air base newspapers, an exercise that seemed remarkably well matched to my background.

Journalism continued to feel approximately right after the war. The romance had faded out of daily journalism, as I looked back on it. I had worked on a morning paper, mostly on night shift. That was not much fun, particularly since I had gotten married to that wife who was worth coming home to and by this time had a child in the same tradition. Just as I was discharged, I got the offer of my old job on the trade journal back. It sounded good to me, so back I went, with more pay and a few more perquisites.

I plugged faithfully at the trade journal job. Indeed, I did turn out to be a fair journalist after all, but my interest in the subject matter again began to wane. I revised some of my self-impressions during these post-collegiate years. First of all, I discovered I was not really lazy—just spoiled. Secondly, I learned that I had stronger intellectual interests than my three full-time years as a college student had revealed to me—at least I am stimulated by an academic atmosphere. Thirdly, I learned that money, while a source of some satisfaction, is far from being an overweening passion with me.

I picked up these altered views of myself largely by going back to night school "to complete my education."

Self-Indulgent Education

For seven years I attended a university several evenings a week and studied weekends. It was nothing heroic, and I discovered it pleasured me much more than it gave me pain. I received my bachelor's degree and then my master's degree. Above the B.A. level, the schooling was perhaps self-indulgent, at the expense of family. I was taking the work in English Literature which was, after all, not particularly directly relevant to my day-to-day work, but something of a nice contrast or enrichment.

I had the option to go on into a Ph.D. program in English, but it was unthinkable that I jettison my family responsibilities for such a diversion. Instead, I contrived to change work fields to provide me further intellectual stimulation.

A Switch to Advertising

The chance came for me to switch my writing locus from trade journalism to advertising copy writing in an agency run by a business acquaintance of mine who headed a firm that specialized in insurance advertising. A natural transition, I thought.

The advertising agency business satisfied the current need for novelty. It provided participation in a form of art, albeit commercialized and stylized. It seemed less anonymous than the kind of journalism in which I had been engaged, where it fell a reporter's lot to make something coherent out of another person's jumbled thoughts. Journalism was just pulling out of its time-honored scribal function of putting literate words into half-literate mouths.

Name Up in Lights

Away false anonymity and modesty! The new career got my name in the small firm as a partner, and that pleased me. I was feeling the first prickings of those identity stirrings that characterize mid-career attitudes. To see one's name in lights, so to speak, is something of a cure for the obscurity blues.

The advertising agency phase was a good transition. The better pay was welcome. It kept up the continuity of writing in a financial area, and yet I sold new business for the agency, hired and fired people, and discovered some talent in these less than artistic endeavors. This was a transition, but from what to what I did not know. Then I found out.

It started at a cocktail party, where I met a Roman Catholic priest. No, I did not take Holy Orders, but I did undergo something of an unwitting conversion. The priest was the dean of the business school of a local Catholic university. Without much urging, I unfolded to him my enthusiasm for education and the fact that I was just completing an M.A. degree. Had I ever thought of teaching? Well, yes, one couldn't go through ten years of university level schooling without picking up a little chalk in the blood.

"Would you be interested in teaching an evening course in advertising?" I heard the dean ask, and I asserted that I would. Thus, in happenstance fashion began my long work affair with higher education.

My first few years of collegiate teaching were interesting, if a bit split in personality. You see, I kept one foot in advertising agency work to help support us even when, subsequently, I crossed over to full-time teaching at another university. After four years of that, during which I had a growing affection for teaching at the graduate (M.B.A.) level, I became the administrator of an M.B.A. program as well as a teacher, leaving the advertising business altogether.

I had been a businessman, so administration of an academic nature made more sense for me than it would have for more traditionally trained and research-oriented professors.

I had come to a period in which the autobiographical analysis I have been unfolding here served, together with a Career Plan and a Log of Events, to help me organize my further progress.

Another Stock-Taking Device

For some people, these would be enough checks; for others, perhaps overkill. However, for the careful person, another useful device can be that of having someone else write a critical summary of your career—or at least sit down and read or patiently listen to your own autobiography. Such a person preferably is somewhat experienced in the world of work—not necessarily a personnel specialist. Such a person obviously should be facile enough with words to write or talk about his or her view of your career. It can be a friend, but not a rival. You and such a person should like and trust each other. You can pay or not pay such an alter ego. In most cases, the reciprocal exchange is worth its trouble.

Your biographical alter ego can be a useful person with whom to share ideas, on paper or otherwise. The reciprocal idea grows out of exchange interviewing and resume writing shared by business school students to help one another. It is a time-honored form of direct cooperative effort.

Spouses as Biographers

Some people derive great support from their spouses. I was in that category. My wife and I have never been rivals. I could not have made the searching forays in early mid-career without her support. There is more on this form of complementary effort in chapters involving dual careers.

Third-Party Referee

Events tumbled along in a succession that seemed to require someone else to pitch in in a biographical role that might help me with my decisions. I had reached a point where I needed a reactor—someone to check my plans, my log, and my autobiography in the light of new moves and opportunities.

I had reached a juncture in my career where I could go comparatively little further with my second school as employer. I was a deputy dean and a tenured professor in a modest business school, largely undergraduate and commuter in character. I found myself interested in serving in similar capacities in a much more prestigious school of national draw and dispersion. I scouted around for a bit and fell in with an interesting job offer that seemed to answer my prayer—except for one hitch. I would not be a tenured professor but would do some teaching, and my deputy dean administrative duties would largely be carried on as a placement director of the school. I selected as my confidante for this round a university colleague who was not in any way a competitor. I pressed on him my autobiography and filled him in on additional questions he might have. I offered to play alter ego for him should the occasion arise.

Some Reactive Insights

He examined my autobiography and heard me out. He then told me of his conclusions. Some of them did provide some insights that struck me as sharper than my own.

Whereas I was worried that directing a placement operation was to be something utterly new and foreign to my life, he pointed out that as assistant dean on my current job I was deeply into the placement of our graduates already, especially in marketing, my area of teaching and previous business practice.

He stressed that I had often affirmed to him my feeling that too much teaching blurs or dulls classroom performance and that, as far as I was concerned, more one-to-one advising might vary the pitch desirably for me in the new job.

He also indicated that, despite pretensions to completely democratic attitudes, I was something of a snob and, consequently, he thought I would be considerably happier with more select students, those somewhat older and at a higher academic level than the ones with which I had been dealing.

The Prestige Theme

He reckoned, in corollary fashion, that prestige meant a great deal to me, that money hunger was negligible, since the new job I was considering offered very little more money than my current job.

He told me, "You like the Ivy atmosphere, the ambience of the place, the reflected glory. You like the idea of serving something bigger than you are, some broad or grand institution. It's a wonder you did not become a priest in the first place!"

Well, I took the new job with the bigger-time M.B.A. program on a combination of his advice and my instincts.

Not many months later I had further occasion to wrestle with another career problem and once again consult my indices: The Initial Plan, The Log, The Autobiography, and my biographical confidante.

The New Setting

One of my several duties on my new job was to supervise a large evening M.B.A. program. In this role I helped one of the large banks in the city gear its in-house M.B.A. training program to what many of their students were carrying in our outside program.

Out of the blue one day came an unsolicited offer from a high official of the bank. "Dick, how would you like to join the bank, in charge of all this training? We'll make you a vice-president and double your salary at least. What do you say?"

"I say I am reeling a bit, let me think about it." What I really wanted was a little time to search my soul and sift my plans. My exhibits spewed forth the answer in twenty-four hours.

The answer was "no." "My God," said the banker, "You never even asked what the money was!" My confidante turned the trick by writing:

> You threw away your chances to be a businessman for the schoolroom and the lectern, so to speak. You are incorrigibly smitten with a vision of yourself as the kindly old writer and schoolmaster, at the same time maintaining a third-party interest in business, a typical writer-professor-observer of the scene. You're the kind of guy who rode a bike long before there was an energy shortage, who affects a pipe, and who would wear tweeds in a West Indian summer.
>
> For you, Mr. Chips, it'll never be goodbye to all these academic images. Can you see yourself as a banker in a pin-striped suit?

Once you have found an adviser like this one, never let him go. His sidelong glances into my mirror seemed stunningly accurate.

Self-Exercise

A Critical Autobiography

Sit down and write your own autobiography. It need not be lengthy or detailed, but it should be as honest as you can make it.

To assure greater detachment in assessing your autobiography or any of the devices you have employed as a result of the exercises at chapter endings, it can be wise to present your material to a confidante, an honest friend who can help you assess where you've been and where you are going.

Perhaps you can reciprocate by acting as a referee for your colleague's career planning.

Suggested Readings

BUSKIRK, RICHARD. *Your Career—How to Plan It, Manage It and Change It.* Boston: Caliners Books, Inc., 1976. Good overview of planning.

MONTANA, PATRICK J., and HIGGINSON, MARGARET. *Career Life Planning for Americans.* New York: AMACOM, 1978. Worth a look, whatever your nationality.

CHAPTER NINE

Mentors and Sponsors

No person ever built a career alone. Oh, certain people of towering artistry or inventiveness may have had less dependence on others—clients, patrons, colleagues, parents, or friends—but even Jesus Christ was beholden to his followers for the spreading of his teachings. It is certain that every person who is successful in his own right has been helped there by his associates. As surely as one classic route to failure is to fall in with the wrong companions, the success route is to fall in with the right companions.

It would be brutally self-serving to suggest that associates be selected solely from among the potentially useful. However, an eye cocked to influential or inspirational associates never hurts.

It gets down, on the one hand, to luck. Many people can recall chance meetings that changed a career. My whole second career in academic institutions stemmed from a chance meeting at a party with an academic dean. On the other hand, my second move resulted from deliberately seeking out another dean at a convention and engaging him quite deliberately in conversation.

So much for the catch-as-catch-can sort of acquaintance. It probably goes without saying that the more allies one has on the work site, the better the chances for success. It pays to get to know as many people as possible, and to have some understanding of the various jobs in the place.

Probably the most valuable acquaintances you can make are with older and more experienced people who will take a special interest in you. The role of a true mentor is a subtle and delicate one worth examination.

A truly effective mentor will be something of a cross between a parent and a teacher, but still with a different relationship than either. A mentor is usually an older person in the same line of work or organization. Although mentors and sponsors may be officially assigned to young people, the essence of true mentorship is a *voluntary* interest, a mutual personal attraction.

It is probable that a substantial age difference needs to exist, a difference of eight or ten years or a generational separation.

Ideally, the mentor takes a special interest in the younger partner, imparting wisdom, pushing for preferment and promotion, training, advising, and caring.

Those companies that have formally assigned mentors can be good to join, because whether or not the official assignment develops warmly, the company has served notice of its own recognition of the potentially beneficent uses of such sponsorship. When official-assigned responsibility is present and informal warmth is not, the form of sponsorship that occurs may be better than no guidance at all, but it is far from the ideal about which we are talking. Usually, a mentoring relationship is between only two people. Probably, after a few years of intensity it weakens and may die altogether. The mutual benefit lessens as the fledgling grows less callow. It appears that most such relationships seldom go on beyond the age of forty for the younger participant.

For mid-career people well into the thirties, playing a fathering or mothering role can be a rich experience. One learns a concern for others and often sees his own life more clearly when occupying an instructive role.

The same graces that are derived from any teaching experience apply. The teacher must perforce examine his or her own life, extract from it the principal values, order priorities, and light a path for future directions.

There is the warmth of appreciation from the protégé, the feeling of satisfaction from having molded a young career, of having thus passed on one's contributions to a younger generation, satisfying—in that sense—the need for immortality that we all have.

For the protégé, the benefits are manifest. The advice is usually helpful, the sponsorship is valuable in gaining preferment and promotion, and the perspective from higher-ups is of intense value.

My advice to any mid-careerist in his or her late twenties or early thirties would be to seek out a mentor if possible.

Mentors seldom are, but certainly can be, of the opposite sex. The sexual element, overt or muted, can enter such a relationship. In business pursuits, there have not as yet been many females in the parenting role. Unquestionably, this fact will change with the increasing number of women in responsible positions.

Finding a mentor has elements of chance in it, but chance can be helped by sensitivity and alertness on the part of the younger beneficiary in carrying on a hunt for a mentor.

The relationship of Alice Johnson and Toby Welch is a fairly classic example of the advantageous aspects of mentoring. At the same time it points out the difficulty in extending such a relationship beyond its natural time.

Toby Welch had gone to work for the university somewhat by default. A gangling and shy young woman, she had not been successful in the placement derby during her senior year at the university. She had taken a degree in the undergraduate business school with a major in finance and a minor in accounting. Her grades were modestly good, but not strong enough to overcome the negative force of her appearance and personality.

So, she applied for a job as a junior financial analyst through the personnel office of the university and was granted it in the face of minimal competition. As is, unfortunately, the case with academic institutions, the pay was low. However, the ambience was favorable. Toby loved the gothic feel of the university buildings, the appropriate greensward and ivy. Being a mildly intellectual person, she enjoyed the various cultural events offered at low cost on and near the campus. She could go along leading a pleasant semi-student life among various friends and acquaintances made while in school.

By her own admission in letters to her mother, "My life is not exciting, but it is comfortable."

One of her outside interests was the theater. For a time she acted in amateur plays, but was usually assigned minor roles since she lacked something both in attractiveness and in innate acting ability. By the time she took the university job, she confined her thespian activities to a play reading group.

In this group there was a thirtyish couple named Johnson. On play reading evenings, Toby struck up an acquaintance with the Johnsons who, it turned out, also lived in her apartment building.

Mixing with the Johnsons was pleasant, and they would drive her to and from the play readings. They fell into driving together or drinking cocktails together at other times during the week as well.

Alice Johnson held the fairly substantial job of assistant controller of the university, while her husband was a tenured associate professor of biology, on his way up.

Alice took it upon herself to awaken some interest in Toby in moving upward from her obscure position. The older woman held a master's degree in accounting, along with a law degree, from the university. She induced Toby to enroll in some part-time business schooling and, when the opportunity arose, was pleased to slot Toby into a position in the controller's office. Next step a year later: Toby became first assistant to Alice. The younger woman learned a lot. Alice gained an assistant in whom she felt she could invest full confidence.

They both gained from the arrangement. Serious and sustained help was hard to find on campus and, as Alice moved up, she had more and more of a need for a trained assistant. Toby, in turn, worked almost on a day-to-day basis with the president and other people high in the administration.

She moved very swiftly upward through the usually slow bureaucratic hierarchy of the school and found herself directly below Alice in rank.

A new president ushered in a new regime at the university and a new controller was brought in. This was particularly galling to Alice, who had expected the post.

Toby fared well with the new controller. Her modesty and industriousness impressed that gentleman and he named her an assistant controller, equal in rank to Alice.

Subsequently, the Toby-Alice alliance weakened rapidly. Toby stopped seeing the Johnsons and became more and more absorbed in other friends. "I think Alice is jealous that I caught up to her," she wrote her mother. "I think I've become her rival."

For her part, Alice was heard to comment that Toby had "grown too big for her britches." The mentorship was over. Alice moved to a higher post at a nearby university. The two women saw each other now and then at professional meetings. They were cordial to each other, but the old warmth was gone.

A common phenomenon is the stage where the mentor can do nothing more for an apt pupil except move aside for the junior. This is usually the termination point.

The chick should know when to fly on its own wings. The parent should know when to push it out of the nest. However, human relationships are seldom as instinctual as those of the lower animals.

Self-Exercise

Searching for a Mentor

Draw up a list on the form on page 57 of people within your current organization who you think would make good mentors.

How might you attract their favorable notice? You might devise and propose a special project to perform for them.

Are there chances to speak to them at company parties or other events?

Can you devise a relatively nonobvious excuse for seeking their advice? Remember, most people are flattered by being asked for advice.

Do you share a sport, hobby, or activity with a likely mentor—something that will throw you in with the prospective benefactor in a nonbusiness pursuit?

	Yearly Record	
FILL IN PROSPECTIVE MENTOR'S NAME	WHEN APPROACHED	HOW APPROACHED

Suggested Readings

LEVINSON, DANIEL T. *The Seasons of a Man's Life*. New York: Alfred A. Knopf, Inc., 1978.

SHEEHY, GAIL. *Passages: Predictable Crises of Adult Life*. New York: E. P. Dutton, 1974. The interweavings of marriage partnership and careers are treated at considerable length throughout the book.

CHAPTER TEN

Career Switchers

Pervasive in the overwhelming body of relevant comment produced by Peter Drucker on managerial careers is the theme that people may require more than one career to fill their lengthening lifetimes. Change of career is quite different from a mere change of jobs.

Part of this need to change careers may spring from swiftly altering technologies that render old techniques and careers obsolete. A good part of it comes from the fact that individuals reach a plateau of competency in lines of work that are not that demanding, so that the "knowledge worker," Drucker's term for the white collar group, becomes bored and disinterested. He or she may, as we suggest in another chapter, be able to enrich his or her life with hobbies and outside interests, but for some this will not do the trick.

The plain fact is that for many the ache will not be satisfied until and unless the void is filled by another line of "real" as opposed to "play" work. Yet, such a change in careers at twenty-five, thirty-five, or forty-five is increasingly difficult, and not necessarily fulfilling.

As we have observed elsewhere in this book, society (in the person of employers) has a way of punishing those who attempt fairly strong changes of direction in their work lives. It is hard to retrain oneself and then to break through the crust of an established profession.

Many of the attempts to change indulged in by "knowledge workers" may come as a result of their being resentful of organizational roles, by their instinct to be the independent professionals, which they are not. This will often manifest itself with comments such as "I don't mind the work, but I hate the politics of the place." These are individualists who want to rely pretty solely on their own efforts, rather than on group efforts. Or, they may merely be those who have failed at the game of politics and are thus disillusioned and ready to chuck it all.

It can be that what is called for is a change in attitudes, rather than a change in career, since the latter offers radical surgery that can fail.

John Sinclair is a case in point. John was an Episcopal priest at the time I met him. For two years he had presided over a parish in an upper middle class residential community. "My kind of people," John said of his parishioners, and he was right. Clean-cut, well-educated, and proper they were—and well-bred, like their dominie.

John had grown up in a suburban environment, had done moderately well in school, and was admitted to Princeton, a school that his relatively affluent father was pleased to afford.

John's college record was not particularly distinguished and, when he graduated, he did not contemplate going on to graduate school. Instead, he took a job as a salesman for a steel manufacturer. The part seemed to fit his general engineering undergraduate background and his smoothly extroverted manner.

After two years John concluded that he might forever remain in sales if he did not do something to alter his course. Besides, he was beginning to be bored by the work. So, he enrolled in graduate business work at the Wharton School of the University of Pennsylvania. He enjoyed the schooling and found himself a much more conscientious scholar than he had ever been before.

Graduating with an M.B.A., John became a junior marketing manager for a home appliance manufacturer. His duty was to plan promotions and sell them to dealerships throughout the country. Some of his targets were company-owned stores and others were independent department and appliance stores that handled a variety of brands. John's work went well. Soon he was promoted to national sales manager, with hegemony over the entire company.

As he continued to criss-cross the country in jet planes on his job, John had time to read and to think. Gradually, his reading and thinking became directed by an outside interest of his. His wife had introduced him to a discussion group for couples at their local Episcopal Church. The group met every Sunday evening for a discussion of assigned reading, led by the local priest or by a professor from a nearby theological school.

John's comparatively newfound interest in reading and study was much stimulated by the reading and discussions of the church group. For intellectual more than religious reasons, these sessions became the high-point of John's week. He read everything assigned and went beyond whenever time permitted. He was amazed at his growing interest in philosophical and theological readings.

At the same time, the pressures of his job continued to be strong. A national sales manager is like a big-time athletic coach. He needs to win every game. The pressure was always on and he was always on stage, shoring up his sales empire and inspiring flagging spirits. He said to his wife, "I am shagging day-in and day-out, yet I'm not sure for what. All I know is that except for times with you and our Sunday evening group, I'm not very happy."

"Why don't you talk to Father Paul about it?" his wife suggested. He did just that. Father Paul listened to his story. "Do you think you'd like the priesthood?" he asked.

"Yes," answered John, "I've often envied you your career, but it's too late for that, isn't it?" Father Paul assured him it was not, and shortly thereafter John entered a special compact training program at a seminary. This program was designed to admit men such as John into the priesthood rather rapidly. John used up all his savings during this time, but he was happy.

Two years into a parish assignment, John was somewhat less happy. He was busy raising money for a new church building. He seemed to have a meeting every night. He had little time for contemplation or study. At one point he said to his wife, "Honey, sometimes I wish I was a sales manager again. At least I had some time to myself on airplanes."

"Nearer my God to thee," sighed his good wife.

Marvin Mann had always vowed, "Someday I'm going to teach." This is a comment one hears from many people, but few are really willing to make the vow a reality.

Marvin was forty-four years of age. He was a very successful life insurance agent. His clients were both individuals and businesses. His specialty was complex arrangements covering principals of smaller firms where death could scramble the business.

Marvin was an economics graduate of Macalaster College in St. Paul, Minnesota, and went into the insurance business shortly after a stint in the Army.

In his first few years in the business, Marvin worked hard and also studied hard to win a Chartered Life Underwriter designation, an educational accomplishment of some prestige in his industry. For six recent years he taught in the local C. L. U. program at one of the universities. He enjoyed the teaching experience enormously.

One day while working on estate plans for one of his clients, Marvin began doodling some figures appropriate to his own estate. He suddenly realized that, with the renewal commissions life agents get for many years after they have sold an initial policy and with the judicious investment of his remaining assets, he could make it through the rest of his life with little, if any, business activity.

The thought titillated him, and gradually a question occurred to him. Why not take a couple of years off, pick up some advanced schooling, and get into the teaching of not only C.L.U. classes, but other disciplines as well, on a full-time basis?

Thus emboldened, he closed his office and enrolled in the full-time M.B.A. program at Northwestern University. He steeped himself in finance, with a view toward teaching when he graduated. However, he eventually found that an M.B.A. was not credential enough to get anything other than a temporary instructorship at a junior college or at a remote and tiny four-year school. He rejected the latter because it would cause too much discomfort for his family.

He began teaching on a temporary full-time assignment at a city junior college. A few of his students were genuinely interested in the subject matter of basic economics or basic finance. Most of the others could not care less. "I feel like a sitter for grown-up babies," Marvin said to his department chairman one day. The chairman replied, "Like I've been telling you, Marv, your only solution is to get on with a four-year college or graduate school, and for that you need a Ph.D."

Marvin wanted to teach, not research, and the Ph.D. work did not appeal to him. However, he gritted his teeth and applied to Ph.D. programs. The only one of any standing that would accept him was located in another city. Most of his other choices seemed to consider him too old to begin the lengthy process. Marvin quit his job, moved to the other city, and began his Ph.D. work.

Much of the Ph.D. work was onerous for Marvin, but he found some of it quite absorbing. Fortunately, he developed a dissertation topic that caught fire with his professors and with him. In a comparatively short three years, he had the Ph.D. in hand.

His first job after receiving the doctorate was with a state university —another move. It was a fill-in post for a year, and not on the tenure track. There followed a pair of additional temporary jobs. Marvin had a hard time catching on to jobs because he had not had time to publish, and schools were unspokenly reluctant to hire someone his age.

At last, his dissertation was published in a modified form as a book. Marvin got a job with a good state school and when last sighted seemed assured of tenure there. He was heard to say, "I now have what I want and am happy. It's ironic that retirement is just over the horizon. I'd like to have forty more years in Camelot."

While Marvin went from business to education, as I did at one time, movement in the other direction is much more common. So many people in education agree that it is a shrinking industry. Company personnel offices and schools of business are flooded with applicants with two or three degrees and a competency in teaching the humanities and social sciences. There are virtually no job openings in these areas. A tragic occupational overdraft and waste has beset thousands of talented and hard-working people.

If, by necessity or by choice, you should want to change careers, what is the best way to do it? The answer is to research the proposed new career in advance. Seek out people already in the proposed new career. Go to the professional or trade associations, seeking information. Find out realistically, by inquiring of people, whether or not the new field is a truly greener pasture—or an illusion. Remember, one can change jobs, but that does not change skins. If you are running from yourself, you will eventually be caught.

Self-Exercise

Planning
a Career Alteration?

1. First step, talk with as many people as possible who are already in the work to which you aspire. Talk to their trade or professional associations.

2. Is there room for you, or is it an overcrowded field? Don't romanticize if it is a tight field. There is little reason to believe that you will be the one to get the job while others starve.

3. Can you afford the time and money needed for regearing yourself? If a considerable amount of professional education is called for, can you take it? Can you pay for it?

4. What traits are necessary for success in the new vocation? Do you honestly have these traits?

5. Examine your motives for switching. If most of it is sheer vanity or self-escape, be suspicious of such motives. If you feel a genuine calling, that's different. Try always to find ways to do what is both the closest to your heart *and* within your reach. Careers can originate in dreams, but they are hard bits of reality in implementation.

CHAPTER ELEVEN

Sticking with One Employer

A comparatively large number of managers stick with one employer for better than five years after joining the company. Another sizeable group are lifetime employees of one company. These people are unheralded by the press. They aren't the kind of news that stories about frenetic job transferring make.

Speaking as one who has attempted to monitor the whereabouts of graduates of a major business school for nearly two decades, I am always surprised at how stable early job contracts often are. Knowing the tenuous circumstances that accompany the first job out of school, due largely to lack of information, I am always surprised that so many such connections last. It's rather like marriage. Given the information gap that precedes many marriages, I am surprised not by the number of divorces but by the number of marriages that survive.

Of course, Americans are nowhere near the Japanese when it comes to company loyalty. A Japanese worker at any level generally stays with the same company until retirement.

There is afoot in America a strong feeling that company loyalty is passé, that it necessarily inhibits career progress. This has yet to be proven by research. Successful thirty-year careers spent entirely in one company are not uncommon. A surprising portion of the country's chief executives and chief operating officers are home-grown; that is, they have come up through their own companies. A good many companies—Proctor & Gamble is a good example—draw their future executives exclusively from inside, without feeling that they have grown stale or insular in the process. The Japanese corporate hierarchies are among the most successful in the world.

The question of loyalty to an employer is, of course, not an abstraction. It depends on whether the employee thinks he or she is doing as well as he or she could do elsewhere. But that is a subject for conjecture, and usually not one for which the answer is known.

Certain it is that loyalty to employers has decreased over the last half-century. To quit a job in the early part of the century was regarded as a sign of both instability and a lack of appropriate gratefulness. Employers were much more paternalistic in attitude. Witness George Pullman, who created housing, shopping, churches, education, and social events for his employees in the "model" industrial village abutting his plants in Pullman, Illinois, at the turn of the century.

We have come to mistrust the Pullmans and the Henry Fords of the world. We see them as stifling would-be fathers who are the death of individuality among their workers.

Modern companies have grown so huge that it is impossible for their leaders to exert the same head of family role they once played.

The whole notion of professionalism engendered by business schooling has rendered the modern executive more of an independent professional than he has ever been before. The present-day executive tends to measure his progress against his fellow professionals in other companies in the same way that academics do. His loyalties and rivalries are within his craft or profession. The idea of a strong bond or affection for any one institution is foreign to him. There is a tendency, thus, to breed a race of professional itinerants who move from employer to employer as bees move from flower to flower. Some cross-pollination is a desirable consequence.

By and large, one can't say for sure that all the consequences of strong job mobility are desirable. It depends very much on the individual so involved.

Among the possible negatives are the feelings of rootlessness engendered by too frequent moves between jobs.

Ivan was a highly sought after manager of electronic data processing. His skills and experience were universal—that is, they could be applied to almost any sort of company or institution offering any kind of product or service. He was not product-bound, as are so many specialists. As Ivan was wont to say, "Computers are computers, regardless of what use they are put to and where."

He could and did move with ease from company to company in an upward spiral of wages that was almost dizzying. However, by the time he got to me he was dizzy himself. These were his opening remarks: "Dick, I have lost a sense of identification. I am not personally involved in the fate of the companies for which I work. What does it matter to me if they fail or succeed? I go on to the next company and work at its problems in a detached way."

"But isn't a certain amount of detachment something to be valued?" I asked.

"Up to a point perhaps," he replied. "But I've gone beyond that point and now have no goal greater than my own ambition. Actually, I am not that much of an egotist. I am a man with some need to find something greater than myself, a cause that stands shiny and bright by itself. But I can't find that cause. Part of the problem is, of course, that I have never given myself enough time on a job to develop this affection or strong affiliation with an employer. I am missing what I want, and what I think I want is a passionate devotion to a job that is also a cause. I lost that after I left my first job."

For his first job, Ivan had worked for a big computer manufacturing firm. It was a company that stressed corporate loyalty. When he first joined the company, it had a pep song and a dress code—white shirts, conservative ties, and wing-tipped shoes.

"I resented it a bit," Ivan said, "but more of me really liked it. This was *my* company, one of the greatest in the world. It was practically my religion. Since then I have literally found no anchor for my faith. I think you gather that I'm lacking any purpose. I'm seeking a feeling for something bigger than a breadbox, bigger than a computer."

"My mobility has played hob with my family. I have uprooted them again and again. We have traveled from one end of the country to another like gypsies. One thing we've discovered is that we can live anywhere if we have to. We no longer want to have to."

As people such as Ivan grow older, they often exhibit less affection for sheer money and material goods. They seek other values such as education, leisure, non-business travel, and psychic satisfaction.

Mobility may bring happiness to some restless souls, but to many more it means trauma. Thus, some job switching may be done to stay put. The reluctant employee does not wish to be transferred elsewhere, so he joins another company in his home city when faced with a move. Such defensive mobility is not uncommon, since there is more resistance to circumstances that alter life style than there used to be. As a consequence, many companies are engaging in less personnel transferring than they once did.

In switching from one employer to another, one sacrifices certain pension rights, working relations with old friends, and perhaps the warmth of feeling for the cause. In cases where the transfer is to another location, there can be a substantial price paid by the family.

Self-Exercise

Mobility Index

Ask yourself these questions by filling in the chart below. If the answers are "yes," job switching may not bring you much satisfaction beyond monetary gain. When in doubt, stay put.

QUESTION	FILL IN YOUR ANSWER
Am I habitually conservative rather than restless?	
Do I have strong loyalty to my present organization?	
Do I have strong financial equity in my present organization?	
Do I have a hunch that a move will not be worth the trouble?	

CHAPTER TWELVE

Remaking Homemakers

The woman who seeks to transfer from a home-based career to a business or institutional one is increasingly in evidence. She has been devoting her time to home and family and/or nonremunerative work and hobbies. She may or may not have children. When and how should she embark upon a new occupational stream once she has decided on such a move? This question reverberates hollowly down commercial corridors, since most of the answers growing out of any widespread experience are yet to be formed. Some women have always made these moves, but in relatively small numbers until recently. In the past they were often women who had earlier left fairly formal professions. Such returnees could usually ease back with the help of their professional associates.

The women who have had less in the way of a shaped and applicable past face a greater dilemma. Employers offer comparatively little help, because their own experience assimilating such women is still fragmentary. Frequently, the employers are as baffled as the applicants themselves. Some principles are beginning to take shape through the mist, however.

For the ambitious woman with little prior applicable experience seeking an entry to a job with long-range career implications, the message seems clear that the younger the age at which she makes such a move, the better her chances.

Employers of people of management potential wear future-focused glasses. When they look at a person, they see that person today, yes, but they are also trying to puzzle out what that person will be like ten, fifteen, or twenty years hence, and what they expect that person may be doing for them then.

The Long View

The longer the horizon of potential usefulness, the more interested employers will tend to be in such a potential human acquisition.

Persons above the upper early mid-career line of forty may well be forty-five before they are perking at full value; they may be retiring within five years.

The older one gets, the harder it is to assimilate that person in the pension system. The older one gets, the harder it is for that person to absorb training or to bear going through training with a group of comparative youngsters.

Women who are sighting in on entry level jobs at mid-career are wise to aim for posts that do not require a long training period and for starts that are not particularly popular with younger entrants.

An Entry at 37

Janet Hurley was the wife of a tenured university professor of her same age whom she had met in college. They had married upon graduation, and during the years of his advanced schooling she had held secretarial jobs to support the two of them. She was armed with a B.A. with honors in history and moderate typing and secretarial skills. Janet quit her job, because she was pregnant, shortly after her husband took a junior faculty post. Three children later, when her widowed mother came to live with them, she felt her home was well covered and sought to return to a professional form of salaried activity.

Employers were polite but uninterested in offering her anything other than secretarial jobs. Several suggested that she return to school and take an M.B.A. degree to arm her with a stronger ticket, more appropriate knowledge, and a better perspective of opportunities. She had always liked school, and had been proficient in it, so she enrolled in a full-time business graduate program at her husband's university.

All went well enough until the second half of her two years in the M.B.A. program. She interviewed, without success, some fifteen companies who came to the campus. Once again, all was politeness. Employers greeted her with a species of uneasy solicitude, but with no real encouragement.

In some alarm she arranged an appointment with one of the business school placement counselors, a woman who had returned to work after rearing a family.

"I am getting nowhere," Janet told the counselor. "Employers don't seem interested in me. Is it my age?"

The counselor did not reply directly, but asked her what kinds of jobs she had been interviewing for. Janet identified banks as a primary interest and indicated that she had been interviewing for bank credit training leading to a career in commercial lending.

"I think that's where the trouble lies," answered the counselor. "You see, you've picked an area for which banks seek to hire much younger people than you, to bring them up through the ranks. One has to start young to make it up through the long pull, and you should aim for something less popular with the younger M.B.A.s."

"Like what?" asked Janet. "I've got a joint major in finance and accounting and am interested in public accounting firms, but I understand they like them young too."

"That's right," answered the counselor, "but the same is not necessarily true of corporate, industrial, or even bank accounting. Many corporations like the stability and patience that they find in older hires. Such accounting jobs can lead quietly to controllerships and other analytic positions."

"That could suit me fine," answered Janet. "I'm not shy, but I am basically a quiet person. Accounting suits my undergraduate training in the sense that it is historical in approach."

A few interviews later, having switched her headset and résumé to industrial accounting, Janet got an invitation to a second round of interviews at a home office, and a solid corporate job resulted.

Some Likely Types of Work

Among the more likely types of work for older people with specific business schooling are industrial or corporate accounting, sales, marketing research, retailing, computer science and computer management, personnel work, office administration, and production or factory management. These are not areas in which there is a great press for entry by younger business school trained people. Accounting, office administration, personnel, and computer jobs are to be found in government and nonprofit entities as well.

For older women coming into the work force without specific business schooling, such areas as office administration, sales, personnel, and retailing often do not demand formal business schooling or much in the way of experience.

It pays for people returning to the work force or entering it for the first time to seek counsel from those with experience in private or public business. Advice is the one commodity most people are flattered to offer free.

As in all other phases of career building, the woman turning to paid activity is wise to aim for those jobs that provide some match with things she has done in the past. The trained museum guide or docent may be quite effective at selling ideas and systems. The leader of a League of Women Voters group can rightly draw parallels with paid public affairs activity. Both might find fruition as employees of private or public business or perhaps for the very institutions for which they have been volunteering their services.

Some Attitudinal Cautions

Those who make the latter transition need to be prepared for shocks. A paid employee is frequently treated less delicately and solicitously than a volunteer.

Other attitudinal cautions are in order for the mid-career starter or returnee. Many employers do not appreciate the self-righteous zeal of women who regard paid work as their new-found ancient and inalienable right. Women late into the work force need to take into account the fact that employers still have the right to choose the individuals they like. Militant or arbitrary attitudes are not likely to charm the older men who still make the bulk of the hiring decisions.

What advantages do older females have in plotting new directions? Chief among them in employer minds appear to be dependability and stability. Such people are usually beyond the time-consuming stages of courtship and childbearing and early child rearing. Older women are held to be more punctual, steadier, and more devoted to work and its institutions than their younger counterparts.

Their employers' biggest worries are about the stability of the family—the question of who fills the "woman's role" if children are involved.

The fact that employers are barred by law from asking questions that probe in such directions does not diminish their interest in them.

Here, as in other job-seeking situations, a woman's wisest move may be to anticipate the employer's frustration on these points and volunteer such comments as: "Perhaps you are wondering what my children will do while I'm working a full day for you. The older two are in junior high and high school and can handle themselves after school. The fifth-grader will go every day to my sister-in-law's house on our same block where she will play with her cousins and other neighborhood friends just as she does now." Few employers can further question such reassurance.

Having been a homemaker can certainly work favorably for those women seeking certain types of jobs. One such woman, after retooling through reschooling, found fruition in household product development for a large consumer good manufacturer. She had presided over a three-child household for many years and had been an assiduous comparison shopper, covering that subject in a news column she wrote for the newsletter of a local consumer cooperative society.

One gets back to the fundamental question emphasized elsewhere in this book: "What is my product differentiation? What have I got that others might want in the way of traits, experience, skills, and education?"

Avoid "I'm Just a Housewife"

Part of the barrier in the homemaker category has been the existence of the "I'm just a housewife" syndrome, a sense of occupational inferiority that continues to plague women. It has been exacerbated of late by the huge numbers of their sex who have returned to work and who have made the stay-at-homes feel noncontributive. The point is, of course, that such domestic careerists need in no way feel ashamed of their roles. They should ideally turn to remunerative work not out of any species of shame or reaction to peer pressure, but out of a real desire to be professional managers or administrators. Of course, economic pressure does have a way of being strongly influential.

Some women who have carried on active careers and then left the work force for the family stages have been able to return to their careers gradually. Bosses are increasingly agreeable to part-time return arrangements. It ideally reserves talent for the employer and guarantees a return to eventual full employment for the woman. This can be especially well managed in occupations in which there can be some do-it-at-home activity, such as writing advertising copy, editing, and certain kinds of business research.

We are bound to see much more of a combination of this part-time and "cottage industry" approach, with perhaps two or more early mid-career women sharing an assignment.

For the woman who cannot return to a former place of work or a former occupation, taking a part-time paid job of almost any sort makes good sense. It enables the woman to gain a feel for paid employment and to demonstrate the seriousness of her intent to work. Part-time work can be a vantage point from which to spot full-time opportunities.

The Part-Time Door Is Open

One of Chicago's larger banks runs advertisements promoting "moonlighting"—that is, working second jobs. Featured are people working such jobs. There is a school teacher who doubles evenings as a bookkeeper. Smiling among the ledgers, he talks on TV about how he is socking away some extra money for his family's future.

Now, whether he is piling up some money or merely keeping his head above water, the ad is symptomatic of the fact that many enterprises are starved for dependable part-time workers. This is particularly true with minority and female hires, and it is no accident that the subject of the bank ad is Black. The strategy employers have in mind is to convert such female and minority people to full-time personnel after starting them out as part-timers.

A reference was made earlier to the fact that there are a few instances arising where whole jobs are shared by two people. For women who feel they have many responsibilities, this can make good sense. The trouble is that most employers cannot be depended upon to take the lead in such new and adventuresome directions.

Two women I know did not wait for employers to overcome such a lag in perceptions. They proposed themselves as a job-share team. Both possessed advanced degrees in English and had considerable teaching experience in English Composition. They were painfully mindful that the inability to write is a major complaint of employers about their employees these days.

At first they presented themselves as a pair of trouble-shooters, working with firms in their area by coming in to help train people with writing problems. They landed a few assignments to put on training courses, but business was quite sporadic. Then they approached a management consulting firm with the idea that they set up a department of communications for the training of new consultants in the vital art of effective report writing. Each of them works every other day. They work in their homes on off days. Everybody happy? Well, so they say.

Auxiliary help is an economical investment for many institutions. Part-timers work for less, ask for less, and are more flexible than their full-time equivalents. They do not demand extensive training and indoctrination and are less likely to expect their employers to solve the problems of their lives with counseling, an elaborate pension, insurance systems, and vacations. If a part-timer does not work out, she is more readily disposable than the full-timer and surely more adjustable to seasonal demands.

Part-time hiring enables an employer to gauge a person over a considerable period without a commitment. If she works out well, chances are a permanent offer is forthcoming, based on a firm foundation of mutual attraction. This is an extension of a well-established prerecruiting technique of hiring promising collegians through the use of the summer job, the internship, the part-time job, or the co-op program.

The Oblique Approach

The woman coming into the job market at early mid-career can approach almost any entity she desires with a chance of finding a part-time opportunity and thus make an oblique approach to a permanent career opportunity.

Naturally, it makes sense for the oblique arrow to be fired into the side of an enterprise in which she has possible long-term interest. Thus, a woman with an ambition to be a retail store fashion buyer might apply to be a part-time worker in a fashion department. Whatever her age and her background, if she works out agreeably a permanent job could be hers at the next assistant buyer opening. The known quantity usually has a better chance to fill almost any opening than an unknown quantity.

Attempting to ride a clothes horse or hobby horse through part-time work to full-time glory, an applicant needs to be armed with enough humility to start modestly and work up. She can be wise to mask the totality of her ambitions at the outset. As in politics, there are many times when a too overt pursuit of a goal can cool the voters.

The part-time oblique is a particularly sound strategy for the woman of light experience or long removal from the fray. It becomes a viable stratagem for any person who wants to break the hard crust of any new line of work.

May Take More Than One Job

It may take more than one part-time job to track something permanent, a gradual working back into the mainstream. Many careers are like old-time passenger balloons: hard to steer and dependent on hot air. One has to try to insure that the permanent job in which she lands is leading to a goal set earlier.

Suggested Hunting Pattern

The following is a job assessment of an actual job applicant. You can use it as a model for drawing up your own analysis if you are redirecting your career out of your home to a new one in the managerial/administrative world.

Job Assessment

Name: Agnes Terrill

Assets: Volunteer leadership
Business experience
B.A. from good school
Sophistication

Liabilities: Brief secretarial-level experience only
Age 36

Logical Targets:	Private or public communications
	Business
	Sales
	General administration
Possible Corrective Action:	Apprenticeship with promise beyond clerical
	Some business schooling
Job Obtained:	Office manager of advertising agency

The Case of Agnes Terrill

Agnes Terrill had been growing increasingly restless and she guessed she was too easily bored. Maybe that was one of the reasons she had drifted apart from her husband. Her two children were in junior high school and were gone most of the day. She had a nice suburban house with lots of room. She also had a lot of time on her hands. Agnes had derived some satisfaction during her married years from certain civic and volunteer jobs. She had been president of her P.T.A., manager of a successful local aldermanic political campaign, and chairman of a sizeable local alumnae association of her college. But she'd done these things once, and once seemed enough. Decisive, crisp, and with a good speaking presence, she seemed to flow naturally into leadership roles—and out of them too.

Agnes had spent four of what she considered the most interesting years of her life in a prestigious women's college that had served as a pleasant extension of her upper middle class background. Mildly intellectual, she had done well in school, particularly in Art History and English.

However, in moments of discontent she would charge that "mostly what I got out of my schooling was the exposure to well-bred boys like my husband and a dubious ability to 'talk eastern' by not really moving my lips when I spoke."

At the close of one of her increasingly frequent moments of self-depreciation, Agnes made up her mind to go into paid work. Looking back over her "career" to date, she could see comparatively little that provided much encouragement. She had, indeed, once taken a course in a secretarial school and had gone through the motions of holding a secretarial job for a few months while being courted by her future husband. Although efficient, capable, and attractive, her interests were not profound enough to impress her employers much at that juncture.

74

Sought a Literate Environment

When Agnes totaled up her assets, she sensed she had some talking to do with people in areas that interested her. Her secretarial job, many years before, had been with an advertising agency, and she had liked the people. On balance, they had been relatively literate and sophisticated—her types. Since much of what they dealt with was a form of art, they shared her affection and respect for all the arts.

"I'm no renaissance woman," she said to a friend over lunch one day, "but I want to deal with people who can talk about something more stimulating than the latest football game."

"One place you may find what you're looking for is in the agency business once again," answered her companion, an account executive for a large advertising agency. He agreed to help reintroduce her to that world.

From that point on Agnes circulated as best she could among agency people and those in such associated activities as package goods brand management. This circulation started with social friends and thence by referral from them to people she had never met. For the most part she found them simpatico to what she represented. Her main trouble was translation into a job of promise beyond what one of her interviewers described as the "well-coiffed poverty of the executive secretarial sorority."

An Advertisement Helped

One day her eyes fell on a small "help wanted" advertisement in *Advertising Age* magazine. It called for a "Girl Friday for a small ad agency; a chance to apprentice for management. Need secretarial skills, college degree, social skills." It was the first ad she'd seen in some time that excited her.

It turned out that two men had been bumped out of an ad agency when the agency lost an account, and they then had set up their own agency. One was a copywriter and the other an account person. They needed someone to handle the secretarial duties, answer the phones, and run the office while they tracked down new business.

"This is a uncertain business," one of them said to her. "If you'll try out with us, learn a little bookkeeping, answer the phones, and type our letters, maybe we'll grow. You'll be a kind of an apprentice, learning the agency ropes. If we all succeed, you'll be one of us, and an eventual officer. If we fail, we'll share that too. This isn't one of those nefarious plots to keep you in secretarial bondage forever."

After some initial wobbling, the new firm found its modest orbit. The office grew, and Agnes became its axis. She scrambled. She took two courses

75

in accounting at night and embarked on a third in personnel. She hired two secretaries and a receptionist and trained them. She eventually presided over the important billing procedures and dealt with clients and prospects over the phone. She literally ran the office.

When last sighted, she had become a corporate officer of the small enterprise, had moved into a city apartment, and had sold her home. But she had a real sense at last of finding a home. Personal involvement—a piece of the action—call it what you will, it had sustained her interest.

Group Easing of the Lonely Business

It's very difficult for homemakers, or any other type of job seeker, to gain sustained help from outside organized groups. Usually, it is a matter of finding one's own way, as Agnes did, to sympathetic individuals through layers of friends and acquaintances.

Judge a School by Its Exit

One advantage of schooling as a preparation mechanism for attempts at managerial career switches is that some school placement offices can supply career support to full-time or part-time students. However, these services vary greatly in quality from school to school. One of the wisest ways to select a school is to start at the exit. What are the placement and career counseling facilities? Talk to the people who work there. Talk to recent graduates. Does the placement office provide support to its graduates, or does it just push them out, forlornly clutching a piece of paper?

A related advantage to schooling as a lever for coming into the job world rests in various women's groups on campus in which students band together to provide both practical and moral support to one another by bringing in speakers on appropriate subjects. One suspects that college graduates of the future will have much better blueprints for amalgamating some periods at home as a perfectly natural concomitant to their careers.

Further Group Supports

Women's clubs, church groups, and business and professional associations can offer some program support to homemakers and women in general. They are worth cocking an eye and an ear to, although they are spotty as sources of advice.

Various testing agencies and psychological firms in an area may be helpful to the homemaker unsure of what talents she has. Some listings of such agencies and test centers can be obtained in the appendix of this book, along with lists of ways to approach individual industrial psychologists and career counselors.

While testers, psychologists, and counselors can be helpful in developing self-analysis for career planning, they generally provide little direction as to where and how one casts out one's nets to ensnare specific jobs.

Employment agencies and search firms are so commercially preoccupied with filling standard jobs with standardly experienced people as to be virtually useless for the housewife trying to enter or reenter the work world.

Sporadic articles appear in newspapers and magazines that are helpful; a few such books also appear. Frequently, however, such materials are slapdash space fillers.

Self-Exercise

Personal Assessment Table

If you are a homemaker, or a returnee to the world of formal work after a prolonged absence, the simple job assessment table shown in this chapter and below is the place to start. Laying out your assets, liabilities, logical targets, and possibilities will keep you realistic.

A quite effective ploy is to take this simple table to acquaintances in the business world and ask them for their help in assessing your chances. You will generally find such people sympathetic to your cause—as long as you are asking them for advice, not for a job. Still, a job is often the result of such circulation.

Keep in mind that job hunting is a people process rather than a set of mechanical exercises.

Fill out these columns				
YOUR TALENT ASSETS	YOUR LIABILITIES	LOGICAL TARGETS	POSSIBLE CORRECTIVE ACTION	JOB OBTAINED

Suggested Readings

BOSTAPH, CHARLES, and MOOR, MARTI. "Career Ambivalence and the Returning Adult Woman Student." In *Journal of College Placement*, Summer 1979, p. 19. Some genuine insights.

SUMMERHAYS, BETH, and WOLCOTT, ANDREA P. "Business Attitudes toward the Adult Woman's Successful Reëntry into the World of Outside Work." In *Journal of College Placement*, Summer 1979. This study underlines the difficulties both employers and female applicants have in relating competences developed through active participation in the business community to business needs, the difficulties such women have in goal identification, and the worry employers have over the "professional attitude" of women with strong family ties.

In addition to favoring training in modern business practice, basic accounting, math, the language of business, and of particular industries, certain largely nonexistent internships were mentioned as a solution to some of these problems. Certain sales training courses, such as those in real estate, were mentioned as general builders of the kinds of sinews needed to sell oneself.

CHAPTER THIRTEEN

Challenges for Women

The biggest career barriers women have faced in the United States have been alleviated by granting them some parity with males under the law and by even granting them some preferential treatment.

The assumption that these actions have solved all the problems of women could be the remaining problem. Legislating fairness will work only part way. Whereas laws may be impressed upon the minds of men, these laws will not necessarily affect their hearts.

There is still a gap between males' professions of interest in female welfare and actual practice. The battle is far from won. It will only *be* won over time—through the successes of women.

Let's see about where we stand. Females represent 52 percent of the United States population and 41 percent of our total force working outside the home. The number working outside the home is calculated to reach 54 million by 1990.

On the more discouraging side, a mere 6 percent of the nation's working women are administrators or managers. Undoubtedly, this figure is rising—even as I write.

Of all board of directorships, only 2 percent are held by women. Women in the private sector earning $25,000 or more a year number 140,000. This compares to 4,173,000 men currently earning that much. It has to be admitted that substantial gains have been made in recent years.

However, in the managerial area the disparities between male and female success rates are great.

One difficulty faced by women has been the need to play catch-up ball in the educational sense. Being capable is sometimes not enough. For example, to be a financial consultant in a major bank, it is necessary not only to be capable but also to have some formal schooling in modern financial theory.

Women have certainly been going to college with regularity, but majors in Art History and English have had a tendency to lead to work in the secretarial pool.

Larger numbers of women have been seeking M.B.A. degrees through part-time and full-time programs. Today, women comprise some 25 percent to 50 percent of the enrollments in these courses, with the percentage higher in the evening courses than the day courses. This would appear to be a recognition by working women that there really are opportunities where they work—if they will prepare themselves for these opportunities.

As a result, however, the woman with an appropriate advanced degree loses some of her unusualness, as more and more of her sisters complete similar programs. One has to adopt the attitude that it is not the degree itself, but the competitive knowledge it signals, that makes the difference in the competition.

Different companies, and different men within companies, have variant attitudes toward female employees. It pays a woman to inquire as thoroughly as possible about a prospective employer's real attitude toward moving women ahead.

A good dictum in any job search is to get beyond the personnel officials. When it comes to women and minorities, personnel people can be all sweetness. They have quotas to fill. It is important for a woman, before she signs up with an employer, to ask to talk to female peers in jobs similar to the one she is seeking to take. This method can produce some shocking testimony or some quite favorable reviews. By talking to more than one woman, one can guard against the possibility of coming upon a nontypical sample of enthusiasm or mistrust.

An increasing number of companies these days are combing the files of their female employees in order to reclassify them and identify them as managerial candidates. This has had a particularly salutary effect upon those thousands of females. Often college graduates, they had been languishing in executive assistant categories—a step above a secretary, a step below a manager. Firms with an executive assistant mentality have to be watched carefully.

Jane Muir was baffled. She had managed to get a job as an assistant brand manager with a large package good manufacturer. But here, two years later, she seemed to be stymied and seemed not to have moved as fast as her colleagues.

She had, early in her career, made a fast friend of a woman in the personnel department, Angela Rossi.

One day at lunch she said to Angela, "Something has gone haywire in my career here. Would you give me a hand in unraveling the mystery? I get good reviews on my work from my bosses. I think I am at least as work effective as most of my fellow assistant brand managers. Yet, for most of them there have been promotions, and for me there has been nothing."

Angela agreed to set out on a discreet inquiry. She asked some of Jane's superiors where the trouble might lie. On two occasions the answer came back, "Jane who?" One of the other answers was, "She seems like a nice, quiet little thing."

Angela strung these comments together, and they presented a profile of Jane's personal effectiveness as being virtually nil.

Jane was unusually small in size and in voice. Although not unattractive if one noticed her; people didn't notice her. A strong part of the modus operandi of her brand department lay in fair-sized meetings in which six or seven people would get together to talk about a brand campaign or a set of problems. Jane was always present, but was lost in the room. The few times she attempted to speak, her voice was overpowered by noisy male counterparts. After a few such rebuffs, she ceased trying.

Jane signed up for a course in assertiveness training in an adjunct program of a nearby university. One portion of the course stressed voice projection. This seemed to Jane of greatest value. Her enrollment in the course was a secret between Angela and Jane. The people in the office meetings began to sit up and take notice when Jane took the floor.

The lack of physical size and the voice strength to fill a room are liabilities for many women. Many are survivors of a culture in which women, like children, were seen and not heard. For some, it takes a real positive effort to change for the forceful.

Another bit of hewing to tradition that keeps women in a species of slavery is the household chores division in cases of dual-career couples. Unless the woman in the equation is unusually forceful, she winds up carrying out the major portion of cooking, cleaning, shopping, and child care. Studies at the University of Michigan show that while husbands do help out with a long list of chores, most are not committed, serious homemakers. Men put in an average of 9.7 weekly hours doing housework. According to the Michigan study, their wives, who also work full time, put in 24.9 weekly hours.

There is strong evidence that women are more guilt-ridden than men over "neglecting" the children. Organizations such as the Parenting Center in New York have developed programs to teach parents not to feel guilty about choosing a career, to give them confidence in their children's love, and to help them understand what quality time with their children can be.

Various theories have been set forth as to why women have not advanced beyond middle management. The strongest part of the answer probably lies in the late start women have had, but there may be other ingredients.

Women executives have commented on the conservation of their sex toward risk, change, fluidity, uncertainty, ambiguity, measurement—in short, principal ingredients of a successful business career. Women are coming to realize that neither complete career devotion nor full devotion to family are necessarily the keys to a happy success.

It is probably still true that a woman has a better chance to move ahead in so called female intensive industries that have long employed a large number of women. These industries include publishing, finance, retail trade, communications, apparel, and the service sections of the economy. Perhaps significant is the fact that the latter section is growing.

The male intensive industries include construction, mining, utilities, transportation, and durable goods manufacturing. One thing you can say is that for women managers, the competition with other women should be considerably less.

Women have a certain advantage over men in the variety of clothing that they can wear, but some women can find this choice baffling. Skirted suits and accessories that are neither too frilly nor too masculine seem to be in order.

The point is sometimes made that women are handicapped when it comes to understanding the nature of the games inherent in business. It is presumed that boys are led to be more game-oriented by training, and that they can understand the rough and tumble processes of business politics that are frequently held to be analagous to football.

Likewise, there are those who emphasize the military nature of the pyramidal business structure and hold that women are less able than men to grasp this picture. However, there is nothing complex in either the games-manship or the military aspects of business hierarchy. It is hard to believe that any woman would long have difficulty in grasping the concepts.

Likewise, one hears that women are less comfortable than men with scientific and mathematical principles (as opposed to literary perceptions) and therefore less suited for managerial careers. Anyone who has seen how well women are doing in current M.B.A. programs would doubt the efficacy of this generalization.

One hazard faced by the career woman is her lack of understanding of men. There is the sexual side and the fairly common phenomenon of the philandering male who considers women's sexual favors his prerogative. Keeping business relationships on a platonic basis is essential to most executive progress. Sexual affairs are too obvious within an organization to go unnoticed.

Another aspect is to understand that men are subject to various age-related crises at 35, 40, 45, and 50. They undergo psychological and physiological strains not unlike the female menopause. A woman does well to be as understanding and as sympathetic to her male colleagues as she can be.

There is no such thing as an iron man.

Today, perhaps the wiser people in both camps are working toward some sort of fusion of success out of both kinds of attempts at successful working and living. Success is coming to have a broader range of ingredients, including family life and leisure time.

While there is still little question that having a baby at mid-career can slow down a female career, some advances have been made toward easing the penalties.

Most employers are no longer ill at ease with maternity leaves of variegated nature. They will keep jobs open, arrange to let mothers come back in on a part-time basis, and make some viable attempt not to handicap the mother in job progression.

At the younger stages, a successful blending of motherhood and career seems to rest with the availability of a reliable and sympathetic babysitter and/or the existence of a viable preschool program.

Self-Exercise

Scoreboard for Women

This chart may help you (as a woman) evaluate your chances to succeed in a heterosexual work climate. If your answers are "yes" they may rhyme with success.

QUESTION	FILL IN YOUR ANSWER
Are you working hard to understand male attitudes?	
Are women being promoted to higher ranks in your present organization?	
Are you avoiding hostility?	
Do you have an open-minded boss or mentor?	

Suggested Readings

CANNIE, JOAN. *The Woman's Guide to Management Success: How to Win Power in the Real Organizational World.* Englewood Cliffs, N.J.: Prentice-Hall, Inc., 1978. A woman executive defines the traits necessary for success.

CURRIN, CELIA. "Women MBAs: Mired in Middle Management." In *Careers and the MBA.* 1980 ed.

FENN, MARGARET. *Making It In Management: A Behavioral Approach for Women Executives.* Englewood Cliffs, N.J.: Prentice-Hall, Inc., 1978. Help to women with such barriers as lack of confidence and negative self-image.

HARRAGAN, BETTY LEHAN. *Games Mother Never Taught You.* New York: Warner Books, Inc., 1977. The author spends far too much time debunking myths and being sensational, but there are grams of truth that can be nourishing to the ambitious female.

HIGGINSON, MARGARET, and QUICK, THOMAS. *The Ambitious Woman's Guide to a Successful Career.* New York: AMACOM, 1975. Ambitious and helpful.

PINKSTAFF, MARLENE ARTHUR, and WILKINSON, ANNA BELL. *Women at Work; Overcoming the Obstacles.* Reading, Mass.: Addison-Wesley Publishing Co., Inc., 1979. First sentence of the book reads: "Experts in the behavioral sciences maintain that the greatest barrier to women's succeeding in the business world is their perception of themselves." Then this work goes on, systematically, to help readers overcome that barrier.

MALLORY, JOHN T. *The Woman's Dress for Success Book.* New York: Warner Books, Inc., 1977. Superficial and cosmetic no doubt, but such is life.

MAZUY, KAY K. *The Managerial Woman.* New York: Anchor Press–Doubleday & Co., Inc., 1980. The critical decision for a woman is whether or not she wants a career in which she has to compete with men who understand the system better.

CHAPTER FOURTEEN

Pitfalls for Minorities

Jim Morgan and Henrietta White, who had been classmates in a graduate business school ten years before, met again at a party given by one of the leading entrepreneurs of their city. Like them, he was Black; unlike them, he was a man of limited schooling.

Jim and Henrietta walked over to a quiet corner to talk about "the good old days" and their respective careers.

"I'm at an impasse of the sort that I'm afraid is all too common among the brothers," Jim began. "I've had five different jobs since I got out of school, and now I'm running out of patience with the current one."

Henrietta replied, "Your comment about having held a large number of jobs being common among Blacks strikes home. Why do you suppose our turnover is higher than that of our White classmates?"

"Well, I suspect we shouldn't gripe, because I'm sure one factor is that we have such a large number of opportunities."

"Yeah, every time I turn around, there's someone dangling a new job in front of my nose. If it's not a corporation, it's a headhunter representing a corporation. You just have to learn to resist temptation a bit, Jim."

"Guess you're right. I've been a real sucker for the Black executive searchers. They're always nosing around looking for ways to move more Black bodies to their clients and thus to make another buck. They always make the grass seem greener elsewhere."

"What's been wrong with the jobs you've left?" asked Henrietta.

"Well, they were slow-moving training jobs—all of them. I never had the patience to see the training through. You know, I wanted a big-shot job dealing with big-wheeling problems—like in all those cases at "B" school where we played at nothing lower than vice-president."

"Heck, you knew that was play, didn't you?"

"Well, part of me did, but another part of me—the romantic part—really believed I'd get into such a job fast. By the way, I understand you've got a really good job now, Henrietta."

"Well, finally. Just two months ago I was made a partner in our accounting firm."

"Wow! I understand partners in the big firms make six figures—and at your age! Will you marry me?"

"Well, I must admit I'm well-paid and also well-married," replied Henrietta. "But remember how low the public accounting salaries were, Jim? And they're still low to start with, comparatively speaking. I've got to admit, I had to grit my teeth many times during the early years as I droned away at inspecting the books of companies in Galesburg and Peoria. I almost quit a dozen times for what looked like more rewarding jobs, but something deep inside me kept me on the straight and narrow."

"You did the right thing, Henrietta. I've spent ten years flitting from one job to another. They paid a lot, but every one of the jobs was little more than a training job. I ran into a headhunter the other day who told me the truth. The truth is that I've never held a real job. It's all been training. He indicated that I was at the end of my string. No longer would employers believe that I was a reliable hire. He warned me that being an educated Black would carry me just so far; then I was going to have to perform. You know, I don't really know how to perform."

Poignant words. Another negative consequence of being a minority person has been underscored by a young Hispanic American. He reported that he was moved up unusually fast in his company—often before he was really prepared. He stated: "They were in such a rush to show the world that they had a highly-placed Mexican-American that they pushed me ahead several jumps before I was really ready. I managed to hang on, but I've known of similar situations in which guys have bombed out under such pressure. Then the employer concludes that Mexicans—or whatever—are just no good."

We have gotten a bit away from an age when minorities were hired as tokens, exhibits up front. However, every minority person has to be alert to the possibility of merely being an exhibit manipulated to salve a conscience or to meet the laws.

Talking to peers will help a minority person get an advanced lead on a prospective employer. Seek out minority people already with the organization and you'll get the feel. Are they merely tolerated or are they treated as full citizens? Are there social barriers? Are signs of the old attitudes still around?

Once again, chips on shoulders are better left off. If a minority, try not to be too edgy; also, do not play the martyr. Seek to understand that there can be resentment over the assiduous courting you may receive. Appreciate that some majority folk feel discrimination in reverse. The possibility of backlash is always present. Your own stance needs to be judicious and dignified, setting an example for all people.

Most of the managerial jobs lie in the broad center of society; that is, they cross ethnic lines. The vast majority of your fellow knowledge workers will be White people. You will need to adjust to their ways in order to be effective, but you can also have an educative influence on them regarding those elements in your own acculturation that may set you apart. Most good jobs lie in the *total* culture rather than in some ethnic enclave.

This does not necessarily mean that jobs are not open within minority cultures. There are minority entrepreneurs, bankers, consultants, and real estate operators. Some of them may be quite viable as career mentors.

It can be valuable, however, for the minority person to have been trained in the broader world before turning to an ethnic business. More than one Black M.B.A. graduate has found this to be true.

I can think of one, for example, who started out upon graduation as an accountant for a Black corporation. He did not find his believability as an accountant very highly regarded by his compatriots. "Now, if you'd been trained by one of the big C.P.A. firms before you came here, we'd listen to you," said his boss.

The upshot was that he quit and joined a big C.P.A. firm. After picking up three years of experience in the bigger time, he went back into Black business, where he achieved both believability and success.

This is another example of the importance of prestigious training to any manager. It offers support to the "start big and trickle down theory" which holds that the first job should be for the biggest entity for which you'll ever work.

A similar effect can be operative in the choice of a college. Very often, the minority person who goes to a minority college does not carry the prestige of his fellows who went to a predominantly White institution. This is not necessarily a commentary on the school, but on the halo effect that carries over from schooling at more prestigious places.

A minority person needs to watch out for stereotypic minority jobs off the mainstream. Too often, he or she is shunted into the sideline job of minority recruiting or an E.E.O.C. compliance. Such jobs place one in a staff ghetto, from which it is hard to emerge.

Self-Exercise

For Minority Managers

If your answers are "yes" to the questions posed and you are a minority manager, some changes need to be made if you are to make it in the interracial world:

QUESTION	FILL IN YOUR ANSWER
Do you carry a chip on your shoulder or nurse a martyred stance?	
Do you seem to be a token in your company?	
Are you the constant recipient of embarrassing special treatment?	
Are you, by way of being, a job hopper?	
Are you made to feel like a second-class citizen where you work?	

Suggested Readings

DUCHET, ALFRED. "Advice to Minority and Women Grads." In *Equal Opportunity,* Fall 1979.

LEE, GARY. "Major Advances for Minorities." In *Careers and the MBA,* 1980.

CHAPTER FIFTEEN

Problems of Men

So much attention has been focused on the problems of women and minorities in work life that some of the difficulties males face are minimized. Despite what many regard as the male domination of the world, many men face decided occupational difficulties related to their gender.

The young printing manager beaten out by a woman for press supervisor doesn't feel that it's a man's world. The bank account executive who lost out to a woman for assistant vice-president is in a backlash mood. There is no social gain for some individuals without a corresponding loss being delivered to some other individuals.

I have been in a promotion board meeting that started with the chairman intoning: "Lady and gentlemen. We have one more promotion to junior officer to consider. I am told that Jim Fisher has the longest experience and a clean record. It is said that Fred Johansen is the youngest and brightest of the lot. Marilyn Murphy lies somewhere in between her rivals in the matter of brains and experience. There is only room for one such post, and there will be two disappointed people. What say you?"

The gist of the decision was really captured by the lone female on the board, the personnel officer, who said: "The feds haven't given us real trouble yet, but out of the 150 officers in this bank, only four are women. Ms. Murphy looks good to me."

She looked good to everybody else too. I talked to one of her male rivals later without, of course, disclosing any of my knowledge on the voting. He had put it together. "My timing was off," he said.

He was absolutely right. Another bank, another year, another industry, and with no really qualified female rivals, he would have been advanced.

Okay, what's a poor, White working stiff to do short of going in "drag" or claiming he's a Cherokee? He has to be careful—that's what he has to do.

The first step is good advice for any pass at any form of employment. Study the employer and the makeup of the firm, particularly the sexual makeup in this case. It is far better to enter a firm with too many females than with none or very few. Government pressures are bound to increase on a firm heavily powered with male managers—particularly one of those very large firms that makes such an excellent target.

In short, at every prospective job change or promotion, what we might call the unprotected male needs to try to calculate the current and the future ratio of female or minority rivals.

Of course, there are those who will point out that the predominant males will lean in favor of their own kind, but this is no longer the dependable gauge it once was.

The roster and lineup are changing constantly, but a worried male could observe those industries and occupations, as well as circumstantial individual cases, where his sex may be an advantage.

We might mention academic counseling at one state of its development. We knew of a crying need for male counselors when nearly all applicants and incumbents were female. The director, a woman, yearned for male applicants to balance out the contingent. After all, more than half her students were male, and all the counselors were female.

Health administrators have in recent years sought more males to go in nursing directions—not as nurses, but as administrators with nursing backgrounds.

Retail store managers are eager for men to balance out some of their heavily female departments.

Further listings of occupations and industries would be fast-changing, inaccurate steps that could be construed as countersocietal in intent.

Chiefly, we would observe—as a result of nearly a decade of placement experience—that some places are good for one sex or the other to work. Whereas discrimination directed against males is subtle and not much of a legal object, it still must be reckoned with by the male mid-careerist today and even more by his young brothers.

We have probably gone through the last generation of old curmudgeons, those male bulls in the woods who called all women "girls" and assumed they were "help." But there are still too many who are clumsy at both respecting women and working with them. Respect and care should go hand in hand.

The surest way to accomplish all this in the interest of avoiding the wrong label can be to think about Patrick Joyce's experience.

Patrick Joyce grew up in a father-dominated household in a heavily industrial district. His "Da" was a tough, hard-drinking foreman in an auto assembly plant who had little knowledge of women or anyone else other than his drinking buddies. Pat picked up a lot of these attitudes by osmosis—just by being around the old man. His biases were further confirmed by his schooling and his skill as a football linebacker that won him a four-year ride through a good all-male university—largely in the company of fellow "jocks."

Pat's initiation to the opposite sex had been, by his own admission, much like his initiation to pretzels. They both added a little zest to an evening of sopping up a few beers.

By the time he graduated and took a job, he was even less gracious to females than to all other people. His personality, although open and friendly, was so unpolished that it prevented him for a considerable time from moving from industrial management to the industrial sales job he coveted.

Pat's company made industrial fasteners—objects of varying sizes to hold various types of materials together. "The nuts and bolts of business," the sales manager used to say with hearty, self-approving laughter.

"Gee, Mr. Schwartz," Pat would say to this genial worthy, "Why can't I get on the sales force and off the industrial management line?"

"You don't know people. You're big and dumb and, especially, you don't understand how to deal with women."

The veteran sales manager then proceeded, in his bragging way, to make it plain that sales calls depend on an ability to surmount the walls of two women who are still defending the average target executive. There is the receptionist, often in control of the telephone switches; then there is the personal secretary. These worthies respond in various ways to those attempting to storm the citadels of their bosses. None of them can be ignored.

"Me, I used the old quick joke, the slightly risqué approach. You know, like W. C. Fields or Willie Loman. That doesn't really work any more. These modern women are more professional, sedate-like. And, you know, some of 'em are even in key roles. They press the buying buttons. We gotta' reëducate our people for the new age."

And reëducate them they did. The sales manager arranged, through a counsulting firm, a class in professional sales approaches. As a courtesy, and out of mentor-like affection, he invited Pat to attend. It was not a course that focused on dealing with women in any exclusive way, but with dealing with people, in general. Through the use of video tape feedbacks and live interview devices, the class members got a chance to see how they really looked, a preliminary to improving their social skills.

Attention was paid to new women's roles. Some of it was new to Pat, but a lot of it was familiar to him in a peripheral way even though he had previously shut it out. This is probably true of many males.

The consulting sessions underlined some other points that were helpful to Pat. They pointed out for him the nature of his careless speech modes —the "goin'," "gotcha," and "betcha" patterns picked up from companions, influences, and sheer laziness. Few people in the world of business are charmed by rough-hewn speech patterns from college graduates.

It has become imperative in today's world for any ambitious male to render himself sufficiently smooth in human concourse in general and in manners suitable for types of people with whom he has had little business experience. In the latter category can lie people of other social class backgrounds, people of other nationalities, and the opposite sex.

Thousands of jobs and orders are lost every week by men who say, "He don't" or "Hiya' gal!"

Are these exclusively problems of men? No, not necessarily. However, a number of social snubs and offenses are. We are in a period of heightened sensitivity on the part of women in business who demand to be treated with a new respect. There are no pat formulas to be used, because differing women present differing stances. However, as surely as Alexander Pope declared, "The proper study of mankind is man," we can declare for the ambitious, mobile, male manager, "The proper study of mankind is woman."

Not too many months ago I functioned as a consultant to a large corporation seeking to evaluate middle-level managers. A strong question that emerged was "What are the managers' relations with employees and fellow executives of the opposite sex like?" The majority of our subjects were males, and they didn't come off very well in the perceptions of their female associates we interviewed. It became obvious in that organization that the effectiveness in dealing with the opposite sex was a crucial element in advancing.

The problems that can arise to haunt a male manager fairly early in the game are not necessarily any more numerous than those faced by women. Perhaps it's just that there has been more of what we might call psychological biology focused on the male sex. At any rate, some understanding of common psychological and philosophical states that are markers in many men's lives is of value.

Physical and psychological turning points in men do not necessarily coincide with the timetables for managerial progression developed elsewhere in this book.

Once again, Daniel T. Levinson seems to have scored, this time by developing a useful schedule of male life stages.

Most readers of this book will have lived through their early adult transition stage—between seventeen and twenty-two—and will be at least into a phase that Levinson calls Entering the Adult World from 22 to 28. This upper edge coincided fairly well with where we have chosen to start early mid-career. It is at this point that the exploration of choices takes place and at this point that a lifestyle and/or work style is being forged.

It is the age thirty transition stage that may first produce the trauma that always accompanies altering plans or structures. Heightened questioning begins after thirty about the work life and other aspects of the total life to date, confirming set patterns or trying to set new ones. Most men do not enter managerial and supervisory phases before this point. Up to this stage, the life structure is frequently somewhat unstable and fragmented. A true sense of occupation may not yet exist.

The age thirty crisis seems to come to most young male managers. It is the end of boyhood, a symbol of the new adulthood, the stone on the highway marked 30. Once the outer edge of life, and now generally considered the threshold of middle age, the number has long since struck terror in the hearts of men.

An informal study of the 15-year records of the University of Chicago Graduate School of Business alumni placement showed that its heaviest number of advisees lay within the thirty-three to thirty-six age range. When asked what brought him forth, one such petitioner replied, "Why, I'm thirty-five, of course."

'Tis an age of mortality, so to speak. A man recognizes that he is no longer fit for basketball; he is tending to paunch; his hair is receding. His career is partly spent, and his rewards may seem too few. He may be sated with a marriage, or jaded by the overrated blisses of extended bachelorhood.

As one friend put it, "At about age 35, people rather pointedly started addressing me as 'sir.' I was used to 'son' and 'buddy' as my terms of address."

A lot of job trading and mate exchanging takes place at thirty-five or thereabouts. Some of it may be wise, but any man has to try to make sure that his moves have substance, that they are not just frustrated expressions of some sort of premenopausal pique or whim.

Many an employer comes to me with a genuinely baffled look in his eyes and asks why "George" left, and you have to hypothecate that, among other things, "George" was thirty-five and that he lay awake too many nights staring at the ceiling and asking himself, "What have I got to show for busting my back all these years? Isn't there more to it than this?"

There are two answers to such night cries. The first answer is yes, there is a lot more, but you've got to seek it out. The lot more is deep in life—the way oil is deep in the ground.

The second answer refers to busting backs or other parts of the anatomy. To make much of a mark in the world, hard work is more in order than most people imagine.

Getting on to the magic marker of forty, a man is neither young nor old. A lot of his youthful dreams may have faded. He can be resentful of younger competitors. He is worried about his own children and may seem to them tyrannical because of his hopes for their perfection.

At any age, but in the crucial twenty-eight to forty category particularly, fatherhood and family are intense career considerations. This has been documented in various works of art, most notable of which is the film, *Kramer vs. Kramer*, in which a father, whose wife deserts him, tries to juggle a career and a son simultaneously.

The demand for maximum concentration on his career work bites a man at the same time that his growing family needs him. Boy Scouts, little league, P.T.A.—the model American father is pictured as being much involved in such matters.

Family and community pursuits can occupy a great deal of man's time. Here again, most men have to draw some limits and achieve some balances to preserve equanimity on both sides.

Of course, there are the workaholics who, at least subconsciously, vote every time for the job and there are the neighborhood guys who always seem to be around fixing the house and the car and playing with the kids.

Whatever the other necessary ingredients for success, men will quite probably have to work at the ambiguity of dealing with women of various moods and attitudes.

A common approach of the "emancipated" male is to treat women no differently than he treats men. He may find, however, that some of his female "buddies" don't go for being "one of the boys." They regard themselves as still deserving of differential treatment. They are equal with the "boys," but demand some separate treatment in business.

Some similar difficulties can face the heterosexual male in attempting to deal with homosexuals of either gender. Some such people seek to be treated without reference to their sexual attitudes. Others emerging from the "closet" are likely to be fairly strident about their difference.

Does sexual activity have a place in business? The journalists seem to think that it does. "Sleeping your way to the top" makes a popular theme for books and movies alike. There is no place, however, where discretion could be more appropriately termed the better part of valor. Boards of directors are not known to look with favor on obvious "swingers" of any sex.

It is in the thirty-five to forty age range that we find many of the most startling career changes, as well as divorces, taking place among men. I would hazard a guess that career changes are more successful in moving men in new directions than divorces are.

I have personally come across dozens of businessmen who, in the thirty-five to forty period, wish to leave business altogether for what they fancy is a more altruistic and less commercial life.

It is our understanding that one of the major Christian denominations has long found businessmen at this stage of their lives quite fair targets for the priesthood. Some of these men are then shocked to discover just how money-oriented the average parish organization has to be.

At least there grows in a certain number of men in the later stages of early mid-career a generative sense of wishing to serve others. This is just as well, because the path to top-command jobs narrows rapidly at this stage. Jobs of service and mentorship roles are often solutions to these altered focuses. Such a softening of men's attitudes at the older ages can be helpful preludes to preretirement and retirement activities of a generative nature.

Real among the problems men face as they grow older is the problem of the decrease in ability and desire in the sexual sense. Well publicized is the "second childhood" behavior of older executives with assorted younger women. There is apparently a certain rutting madness that has caused many a man to lose his head—and sometimes his job—over "a bit of fluff."

It never lies within any human's province to write dispassionately about sex. However, all research evidence has it that problems associated with it can heavily influence a career.

It is advisable for any man who has problems with this phase of his life to read literature in the field and to seek medical-psychological counsel if the matter seems to be affecting him in either manic or depressive ways.

Evidence is strong that the sexual drive cools steadily in most men as they grow older. Such is not the case with many women, who enjoy sexual activity to much higher ages.

Waning sexual powers drive many a man to seek, rather frantically, to prove his macho nature by seeking stimulation from younger women. A man's psychic and work performance may be affected by his grieving over his loss of sexual powers.

Self-Exercise

For Men Only

Think about your relationship with women and ask yourself these questions.

QUESTION	FILL IN YOUR ANSWER
Do I assume that all women in an office are secretaries and clerks until I am told otherwise?	
Do I order female secretaries and clerks about arbitrarily, rather than treat them as human beings?	
Do I behave self-consciously in the presence of women? Am I unduly fluttered by an attractive woman in a way that alters my ordinary approach?	

QUESTION	FILL IN YOUR ANSWER
Do I attempt to make physical overtures to members of my staff or to other business associates?	
Is concern with my own sexual performance weakening my work performance and generally depressing my personality?	
(Particularly true in taking a new job.) Am I careful to study the mix of sexes in the office to make certain—as certain as I can—that my progress will not be limited by my sex?	
Am I in the grip of the old attitude that women are not equal to their male counterparts?	
Am I fair-minded in my assessments of female performances on the job?	
Do I exclude women from office-related socializing?	
Do I tend to exclude women from policy-making meetings that take place in the office?	

If your answer is "yes" to any of the above, you are engaging in a form of chauvinism that is damaging to you and to others about you.

Suggested Readings

HARRAGAN, BETTY LEHAN. *Games Mother Never Taught You.* New York: Warner Books, Inc., 1977. Marvelous perspectives for men on how not to relate to women are provided here.

LEVINSON, DANIEL T. *The Seasons of a Man's Life.* New York: Alfred A. Knopf, Inc., 1978. Essential insight into the problems of the male worker at all stages of his life.

MAYER, N. *The Male Mid-Life Crisis: Fresh Starts After Forty.* Garden City, N.Y.: Doubleday & Co., Inc., 1978. Recites specific instances of regrouping beyond forty.

CHAPTER SIXTEEN

Dual Careers

Every career in which there is a marriage or a similar living and loving arrangement contains dual career considerations.

In the so-called traditional marriage, in which the woman has been a housewife, there have been two careers being carried on even though the husband's career has seemed the more obvious one. The woman was really only at a stage of her career that was not talked about in career terms. All this is changing.

The basis for any dual career arrangement should be some sort of deep affection between the persons involved. This may have some roots in mother love or in parent love in general. Parents are, to a greater or lesser extent, nurturers and advancers of early career dreams—to a point where at times, of course, they can become dream inhibitors.

The support and cross-mentoring that goes on between a loving couple can strengthen each of them if their being united causes each to be supportive of the other. Such people, special to each other, can render less lonely the assault on the world each must make. The same ingredients of caring and compromise that make for a successful love relationship will allow for a successful career relationship. It's as simple as that.

One can certainly extrapolate from such conclusions drawn from the study of males to heterosexual relationships or homosexual relationships of like character. You are fortunate to find a special person. He or she is fortunate as well, if both use the relationship to mutual benefit.

97

It can be seen that such a relationship, ripening at an early career stage, can be most beneficial, although such support should be welcome at *any* life stage. By early mid-career, one probably has succeeded or failed at founding such a relationship. A recognition of the aspirations of the "mate" can help to improve the feel of the work life for one or both of the partners.

There's a story still unfolding that underlines the give-and-take aspects of so-called joint career problems, along with illumination of the host of assorted considerations upon which a total life together can be built if it is to taste of success to both partners.

Grace and John were from the same middle stratum of society in a small midwestern city. They attended a big state university where they met. It was still an age in which couples married upon graduation and started out on the husband's career. John took a post as a mechanical engineer and his wife, a liberal arts graduate, got a job as a receptionist. They seemed to be off to the kind of start of which their parents would approve.

John got a break in his second year on the job—a chance to work in the Brussels plant—on the strength of some familiarity with French. Grace went along as the dutiful housewife. For a time, she was Cinderella in the fascinating old city. She had never been to Europe before. She flirted with the idea of taking a job, but job opportunities were rare for a foreign woman with little knowledge of French and no knowledge of Flemish.

John did not press her on the job score. Together they took a class in French, but mostly he was very busy and fell into the locally accepted practice of treating his wife as a social appendage. When he referred to her as his "little Dutch doll" one night, she hit the ceiling—and he never knew why.

Not far from Brussels lies an ancient town called Louvain by those who speak French and Leuven by those who speak Flemish. It is the site of an ancient Roman Catholic university that was recently split in two by the linguistic schism in Belgium.

Grace—and sometimes, on a weekend, John—spent a good deal of time prowling the ancient streets and buildings of Leuven. John had once studied under a young Belgian professor who now taught at Leuven, and he introduced them to the local spots of interest such as a statue of a student who continuously poured a flagon of water (in lieu of beer) through his head and a marvelous faculty club set in the basement of an ancient home for unattached women.

Gerrit was this professor's name. He was an American-educated economist, now teaching in the graduate business school of the University of Leuven. A Flemish-speaking school, the classes were taught in English, and the curriculum had a strong American influence.

At Gerrit's invitation, Grace sat in on a few classes, liked them, and one day surprised her husband by saying, "What would you think of my applying for a Master's in Business Adminstration degree at Leuven?" His answer lay on the heavily negative side, but after some sleep and a beer-braced conference with Gerrit, he gave a certain reluctant consent.

Well, it changed her life. They stayed in Brussels just long enough for her to obtain her diploma, and she was ready to assault the management world when she got back to the United States. She was even one degree up on John. He eventually enrolled in an evening M.B.A. program, and she had the fun of helping a male who managed to slough off quite a bit of macho pride. This is often the toughest part of such a relationship.

Grace and John made good use of their nightly social drink (limit two) before dinner to discuss and to plan. Incidentally, the social hour is a lifesaver for many a couple, a good meeting to continue when the couple becomes a family.

The questions during the cocktail hour were fairly predictable. What's new on the job or at school? Should we buy a new car? How about vacation? Am I really getting a maximum kick out of my work life? Should we have a baby? Without a rigid agenda, and in no particular order, all these things would come up.

The baby question was always there. Grace had obtained a good job with a management consulting firm. Eventually, she would be a full-fledged consultant. Time out for a baby would cause some break in that process, especially since there would be travel involved at the next step upward.

John, who had a relatively stationary job as an industrial analyst with a corporation, wasn't keen on the travel idea for his wife anyway. Being with her was, in many ways, his principal recreation, and he was concerned that children would demand too much of her time. What would they do for sitters? And, finally, could they, in fact, have children?

They concluded that they must agree on a course of action and let the process work out. The only way any career-related domestic problems can be worked out is simply to agree on and take a course of action. "You could read books until you were blue in the face, and this is the conclusion you'd draw," was John's comment.

They decided to set the process rolling by trying for a baby. It took a year, but it worked. This hobbled Grace on the job. She did not pass into the consulting stage, but took a six-month leave when the baby was born. For a time it was fun, although a fairly frightening process, being responsible for a new life. Then it began to wear thin as a full-time occupation. She got a fair day sitter and went back to work. However, she was forced to turn to a more research-oriented job than she would have liked in order to avoid a travel schedule that would have kept her away from her child too much. That was her trade-off—to use their cocktail-hour parlance.

They loved the baby and, except for the usual midnight emergencies and vigils, were glad to have her. However, having the baby took its toll on

John's opportunities. This time it was not Brussels but the home office of his company in the East that beckoned. It would mean a better job, more pay, and maybe a chance to afford a house. It would mean more nationwide travel and responsibility as well. It could also mean jeopardy in the attitude of his company toward him in the future if he exercised his option to turn the offer down.

As for Grace, her current employer, with whom she had such a good record, had no office in the new city. It would mean cutting loose from a company that had gone out of its way to help her work around the baby.

These things were a fit set of subjects for several cocktail-hour discussions! Finally, with some trepidation, they made up their minds.

Interestingly, this young couple had developed a trepidation valve that worked pretty well. There was a large French window with a little balcony outside their living room. When they would make a decision, they'd step out on the balcony, no matter how cold it was, and look at the world. Then they'd step back into the living room, close the doors tightly, and embrace. "We turn our backs on the trepidation window," Grace commented. "We then make a determined effort to shut out what might have been and don't talk about it. Some people may not be able to do that, but thank God we can."

Whatever lies ahead, they seem destined for a successful life style, work life, and total life.

Whereas we have emphasized a certain interdependency in almost all careers, we can't overlook the fact that each of us has a life of his or her own, and a trepidation window that we may have to close at times—even on our most beloved friend.

For all the talk about joint careers and career couples, there are all sorts of individual and societal mores that must be taken into account.

We can likewise take books on the various stages, procedures, and crises of life and turn them into self-fulfilling prophesies: "The book says men face a crisis at 35. My God, there's something wrong with me. I'd better invent a crisis!" On balance, it's probably better for people to understand that crises at certain stages, or at any time of life, are not uncommon. Few of us enjoy being too different from our fellows or to be considered eccentric.

One of Gail Sheehy's several contributions to our understanding has been the point that there are substantial physiological and psychological differences in the ways men and women act at various career and life stages. These render joint careers of any kind particularly difficult.

If a couple's objective is maximization regarding an agreeable life together, taking turns in making moves make sense. I have a daughter and a son-in-law who took turns in their early fast-track careers. It sounded great on paper, but the relationship was not a strong enough one, and the egos were too strong for sustaining the marriage.

The necessities for mutually successful dual careers are remarkably the same as those for a successful marriage: compromise, sacrifice, and sharing. Emphasis on *compromise, sacrifice,* and *sharing.* Obviously, many career combinations that look symmetrical to the world are actually quite lopsided when you get to know the people involved.

Self-Exercise

Career Sharing

If you are married (or similarly involved with another person), ask yourself these questions:

QUESTION	FILL IN YOUR ANSWER
Do home relationships take precedence over work relationships? Conversely, does the job take precedence over the home situation?	
Have I had concern in my mate's career that runs beyond the pay check?	
Do we discuss these matters on a regular basis so that I really know how he/she feels?	

Ponder your answers. One can be materially successful whatever the answers, but the personal quality of these successes is more promising if the answers are "yes."

Suggested Readings

SEITLER, HARRIET. "Dual Careers: Managing the Marriage." In *Careers and the MBA.* 1980 ed., pp. 56–61.

SHEEHY, GAIL. *Passages.* New York: E. P. Dutton, 1974.

CHAPTER SEVENTEEN

Main Line Command Routes

Staff and line concepts appear to have originated with the military. Line commanders were men who made decisions and led troops. Staff officers were men who furnished the data and the information on which line officers made their moves and decisions. A person could, in a military career, serve alternately in one capacity or the other.

There was likewise an in-between group of men who could be described as aides, assistants, or deputies to line officers. By virtue of deputized authority, they at times wielded some line power. In business, it is very easy to find parallels to the military. Line officers direct and lead companies, plants, and sales forces, whereas the staff people occupy the more passive role of furnishing the data.

Typically, the major line jobs in business organizations have been in the higher or general management arena, in marketing and sales, and in production or factory management.

Because line management is a clear path to the top of corporations, where the highest rewards tend to be, jobs in this area are preferred over staff jobs.

Of course, there are staff jobs in marketing and production too, and such people as sales managers and on-site production managers are definitely in line for leadership roles.

Finance, accounting, and planning jobs fall in the traditional staff categories. Of course, one can be a line commander of other people doing staff work. such as a chief financial officer. There are some line characteristics in such a job, even though it is basically heading a staff function. Modern organizations are complex enough so that the divisions between line and staff can be fuzzy. Still, some relatively overt and clear line experience is desirable if one is to rise to one of the higher command posts.

The plain fact is that most beginners in the world of business start in staff positions. They are usually not experienced enough to manage anything beyond their own desks, and many aren't very good even at that. The exceptions may be people who start out in sales or in some other form of factory management at perhaps a foreman level. The latter are likely to be engineers.

A staff beginning is virtually inevitable for well-trained graduates such as M.B.A.s. Their schooling brings them up to the latest staff techniques and often beyond the knowledge of the people for whom they go to work. The trick lies not only in getting a good staff job and making progress in it. Rather, it lies in also gaining the requisite line experience to ensure a balance that will lead to upward mobility.

Henry Sebastian, for example, was considered a huge success by his colleagues. At age thirty-six he was comptroller for Latin America for a large, multinational manufacturer of packaging. He lived in a beautiful, company-furnished villa in a South American country and had innumerable other perquisites, including servants and cars. He was respected in company headquarters—someone to be reckoned with.

However, Henry thought he had a pair of monkeys on his back, figuratively speaking. The first was the classic dilemma posed for almost any expatriate, and that was how to get back to his homeland and the head office. Overseas he felt a bit too detached, too cut off from the main seat of power.

He summed it up for his wife, "We are, my dear, really prisoners in this hacienda. I may be here forever more, blocked from a chance to progress."

His wife smiled knowingly and said, "Ah, but what a lovely prison it is, so be patient." She knew Henry, however, and thus knew that he would not be content until he got back to the main office.

The second element of dissonance was the staff nature of his position. If and when he got back, he knew he would undoubtedly be in some sort of controllership position. It was not through a position of this sort that one could become a chief line officer of a company such as this, and that is where his ambition ranged—and at times raged.

The chief operating officer of the company visited Henry's hacienda one evening. In a long, leisurely talk over cigars, the senior man said: "There is only one cure for the staff disease, Henry, and it is a painful one. You will need to step down into some sort of a line position."

"Need it be a step down?"

"Realistically, yes. Any line proclivity you may possess has really not been tested. You'll have to start, if not all over, at least fairly close to the beginning."

A few months later Henry was back once again in his beloved California. He was driving a company car along a freeway en route to his first call as an ordinary salesman of paper boxes for his company. He turned out to be a very out-of-the-ordinary salesperson, developing a superior record of selling paperboard products to industry. He became sales manager for Southern California, then marketing chief for the whole state. A line vice-presidency is clearly a possibility for him.

Another example of transition from staff to the line is provided by Anne Carrington. Ann was hired originally as an industrial engineer by a heavy manufacturing corporation. She operated in an advisory capacity to a plant manager, scheduling production runs. This was fundamentally a staff assignment.

"Back then," as she put it, "I didn't know a staff or a line from a hole in the ground, so I let them talk me into becoming a financial planner. I had taken little finance in school, so they slotted me on to a planning committee to furnish manufacturing perspective to the finance people. I gradually became adjusted to the finance role. I also gradually came to the realization that staff people are usually too hidden from the mainstream of management to attract any attention. Then came my break. The team had a presentation to make to the five top managers of the company. My boss was sick on that fateful day, and I got to make part of the presentation in his place. When I finished, the executive vice-president asked another executive if he knew that girl. I didn't even mind being called a girl in this context, because I figured I had attracted a favorable notice. It turned out I was right. Three days later the executive Veep called me in to ask if I would be interested in being his assistant. I agreed, and thus became assistant to the man who heads the entire manufacturing side of our company. He is on the line, and I am close to it. Actually, I'm in the same job he held a few years ago."

The importance and career value of line experience should be clear to any early mid-career person but, unfortunately, too many people perceive it too late and too dimly. Maybe in the aggregate this is fine, because the number of main line opportunities is limited as one moves up the management pyramid.

The successful line aspirant usually starts staff, moves into line after the first five or six work years, and vaults into a general management post in his or her thirties.

"General management" is a slippery term used loosely by some to describe broad administrative jobs that don't fit the standard functional categories.

Its most accepted usage, and the sense in which we will use it here, applies to higher administrative jobs that embrace supervision over more than one functional category. An example could be the general manager of both manufacturing and marketing in a region. Presidents, chairmen, and many vice-presidential jobs are general management. They involve line or command responsibility.

Higher staff people, such as overall chief financial officers and treasurers, can be accounted general management in some instances.

The vault into general management is the most difficult managerial acrobatic feat to perform. When it is acheived, it is usually accompanied by corner offices, access to the executive dining room, and other privileges.

Failure to perceive the importance of some command experience at a comparatively early age is often the result of disinclination on the part of well-educated graduates to go into what they regard as relatively mundane jobs in sales and manufacturing. People often wake up late to the clean-cut value of the line positions.

Self-Exercise

Hew to the Line

If your answer to the first question in the chart below is "yes," so should the others be if you are to have a crack at line responsibility soon.

QUESTION	FILL IN YOUR ANSWER
Do you aspire to be a chief executive, a chief operating officer, or other high-line officer?	
Have you had any command experience to date, or a good chance of it soon?	
If you are staff, are you at least exposed to higher general management?	
Do you see yourself being given an opportunity to vault above your current specialty to have responsibility over more than one function?	

Suggested Readings

BOWER, MARVIN. *The Will to Manage.* New York: McGraw-Hill Book Company, 1966. Slightly dated but valuable inspirational summary of what it takes to be a chief executive from both technical and personal points of view.

DRUCKER, PETER F. *The Age of Discontinuity.* New York: Harper & Row, Publishers, Inc., 1968. Each of Drucker's many books spends time on the role of the line and staff manager, but this one is outstanding in its several passages on the subject dispersed through the book.

HUNT, F. ROSS. "Specialist vs. Generalist: Who Runs the Company." In *Management Review.* Vol. 64, January 1980, pp. 43–45. The title is self-explanatory.

HUNT, JOHN W. "The Plight of the Manager." In *Work and People.* Vol. 5, no. 1, 1979, pp. 27–31. The writer maintains that the manager's role is declining with the increasing influence of experts and consultants; his direct functions need to be reinstated.

THAIN, RICHARD J. *The Managers: Career Alternatives for the College Educated.* Bethlehem, Pa.: College Placement Council, 1978. The author devotes a chapter to distinctions between line and staff.

CHAPTER EIGHTEEN

Staff Supporters

In a sense, the differences between staff and line opportunities tend to boil down to the old dichotomy that separates the specialist from the generalist. We would stick by the guns fired in the previous chapter to the effect that the highest kudos tend to go to the line officer and the generalist. We would maintain that in most cases it is necessary to start as a specialist, but that it is also necessary to vault above the specialist role to the generalist role before the main career battle can be won. There are those instances where this may not apply. On occasion, someone is advanced precipitously from controller to chief executive officer, but this is comparatively rare. The successful person starting from a controller base will usually make a step to chief financial officer in a sort of mixed generalist and specialist role before the C.E.O. lightning strikes. Surprises are fun, but in management progression, one cannot count on them. Following once again the time-honored thesis that the future belongs to those who prepare for it, those who want to make the generalist leap must consciously aim for it.

Adam Edwards, thirty-eight years of age, was a senior financial analyst. He was paid a whopping salary for the job, one that many a more important sounding officer in his company would envy. He was employed to monitor the expenses of the sales division of a printing equipment company that made and sold large pieces of equipment, such as giant offset presses, costing several million dollars.

Adam Edwards was shrewd. For years now he had kept the sales division on the right track, and expected he would be doing the same for a long time. There—right there—was the rub. He was extremely valuable, and long had been. His future was, in one sense, assured; it was *too* assured. He expected he would be doing the same thing ten years hence. Making more money sure, but the same old job.

The trouble was that he had peaked out at a fairly early age. He had reached the top of his specialty. There was no place else for him to go. When he thought of escape, a frequent thought in those days, he could find no exit. Oh, he could probably transfer to a rival company in the same field, but that would simply be trading like items in what is known in some circles as a "lateral arabesque," or a sideways move of no great value except to provide a change of scene. Adam was not buying that type of move. His solution? As far as he could see, the solution was to enrich the *other* aspects of his life.

Adam's dilemma was the classic specialist dilemma. Rise up fast in your specialty, stick to that specialty, and then there is no place to go.

A brief time ago the placement directors of seven prestigious schools met to discuss their frustrations and the frustrations of their graduates. Major among the latter were the numerous instances they could cite of the tender specialist trap and of those countless instances where their M.B.A. graduates started as specialists and ended there, with no cross over opportunities, so they said, to be anything but super specialists.

Now this is fine for the specialist at heart. For the others, it's much less frustrating if they work for those organizations that provide parallel climbs up the ladder, that offer the rising specialist similar monies and prestige as the rising generalist. Some highly technical companies, heavy in the hiring of engineers, will provide such arrangements. Petroleum companies, for example, will provide parallel routes part way up. However, the highest technical men, engineers, go up only so high. The generalists outstrip them from there on up. After all, how high can a person go and still be in engineering?

Experts and specialists, whether they are in engineering, research, finance, or accounting, do run up against a fairly low ceiling. If they choose the specialty, conscious of its limited potential, well and good. They have done so with their eyes open.

This is not to say that one should automatically try to break out of expert work. Many specialists are temperamentally suited for their roles. It is simply to remind early mid-career people that one pays a price for the luxury of continued specialization. The price paid is limited advancement in the world.

As with everything else, there are trade-offs to be considered, including one's psychological health.

How does one break out of a specialist route? By asking, by pushing, by trying, by suggesting. Education is one of the surest routes, although it does not guarantee success. It seems fair to say that the majority of students in part-time M.B.A. programs, and many in full-time versions, are there to try to convert to generalists—to be managers instead of experts. Engineers, computer operators, and the like can often see no other way out than to attain a generalist degree.

Do their companies recognize the gesture and the achievement? The answer is frequently no. Employers need to be prodded. Often, the specialist has to put on his or her own individualized version of a strike to win his or her point.

How strong is your union of one?

How strong are your traits when it comes to changing your spots? Many a staffer has switched to line only to discover that his or her personality traits are not suitable for direct leadership in a line job. Many a person is promoted into something for which he or she has no skill. A good salesman won't necessarily make a good sales manager any more than a good tackle will necessarily make a good football coach.

Self-Exercise

Given My Druthers

If your answers are "yes" to these questions, don't try to cross over into line management. Stay staff and prosper.

QUESTION	FILL IN YOUR ANSWER
Do you favor long stretches of work time without human interruptions?	
Are you hesitant about making decisions? Would hiring and firing people bother you?	
Are you more shy than bold?	

Suggested Readings

PETER, LAURENCE J., and HULL, RAYMOND. *The Peter Principle.* New York: William Morrow & Co., Inc., 1969. A book replete with examples, both humorous and poignant, of the tendency for people to be promoted into jobs beyond their competency.

URWICK, LYNDALL F. "The Nature of Line and Staff." In *Management, a Book of Readings,* edited by Harold Koontz and Cyril O'Donnell. New York: McGraw-Hill Book Company, 1964, pp. 212–14. The classic delineation of line and staff relationships.

CHAPTER NINETEEN

Senior and Junior Synergism

Inevitably, career focus requires subjectivity. Before anything else occurs, one has to look inward to attempt to discover if the right stuff is there for the career in question.

Preparing for a line of work requires a building of inner resources and skills. There is, however, such a thing as overpreoccupation with career, and that can lead to unattractive self-centeredness. Preparatory accomplishments *can* cause one to be so full of oneself as to render him or her blind to his or her effect on contribution to colleagues.

We heard one man recount an experience he had in the Air Force. This chap had just finished an Officer Candidate course. Everywhere he went the new gold bars on his shoulders reflected the sun of his heightened self-esteem. He was to report for duty to the colonel in command of an air base where he was to take up his first assignment.

Finally, he confidently stepped before the colonel, saluted smartly, and prepared to talk about how splendid he was. The colonel was a short man, and so the nouveau second lieutenant found himself looking over his head at a plaque placed on the wall. Quickly, he read the words: "So tell me quick and tell me true or else, my friend, the hell with you. Not how your glories came to be but what, in short, you can do for me."

110

The motto had its desired effect. It caused the second lieutenant to abandon his intention of bowling the colonel over. He confined himself to answering the colonel's polite questions.

"I have a lot to learn," the shavetail heard himself saying. "I will try to be as useful to you as I can."

The world is full of second lieutenants who forget that there is a long way to go before they lead the troops. Their early assignments, and many thereafter, will be to look after the work of their bosses and to make "the old man" look as good as possible. If this is achieved, their own futures are usually assured.

Every person has weaknesses. The first thing the subordinate needs to do is to sense the chinks in the armor of the chief. This is not for the purpose of disparaging the chief, by carping about his shortcomings, but to help the subordinate bolster the chief's performance.

For example, many a young person finds the older generation deficient in the kind of quantitative and computer-allied analysis that is so possible with modern techniques.

James Ward discovered quickly that his boss was scared to death of using a computer to solve the data problems of a corporate marketing department. As Jim put it, "I was itching from the start to tell the boss that he was nonprogressive, that he was employing far too many people in the manual reporting of data, that here he could use queing theory, there linear programming. I began very slowly and gradually to suggest and to demonstrate the applications of my craft. The trick was to explain matters in such a way that my superior felt in on them. Whenever I went too fast or too far, he put up his back. Progress was slow, but we made it."

Later, the boss confided to a friend, "Jim has been a great help to me—my seeing eye in a dark side of the world. He knows jargon and techniques that are Greek to men of my age. Let me tell you, he often acts as my tutor and I act as his enthusiastic pupil."

Unless the person in charge is a hopeless bigot, most subordinates can find ways to contribute to the consciousness of their seniors. Such is not a never-never land dream. It is an essential reality for those who will succeed. In a few professions, perhaps, the brilliant self-absorbed person may succeed. In most forms of management, even the most clever person needs a subordinate sense to obtain high-level allies.

The other side of the coin will come into usefulness for the man or woman who would succeed. Care in the selection of manageable and contributive subordinates is the key. The bright, but uncooperative, upstart must be trained to be cooperative and useful. Superiors must learn to listen to subordinates and to absorb their contributions without crushing their spirits. The heavy-handed, egotistical "bull of the woods" type of boss will seldom bring out the best in people.

Also, the complementary sense is necessary. Seek out those workers who have talents and knowledge different from yours, those workers who can do the jobs of which you are less capable or those jobs that you do not relish. Fill in the holes.

Get these people on your team. Try to make them not so much subordinates as associates. This will engender in them a loyalty that will draw the best out of them—and out of you.

The desired and achievable effect of all this should prove to be a synergism—a magic interaction between you and your junior associate that is superior to the efforts of either of you alone. It is a case in which one plus one can prove to be three.

Self-Exercise

Synergism

If your answers to the following questions are not affirmative, you need to train yourself to a synergistic orientation:

QUESTION	FILL IN YOUR ANSWERS
Have you assessed your boss's strengths and weaknesses?	
Have you learned from his or her strengths, and bolstered his or her weaknesses?	
Do you value a team feel?	
Do you listen to and learn from your subordinates?	
Do you avoid the temptation to create successors in your own image?	

Suggested Reading

REYNOLDS, HELEN, and TRAMEL, MARY E. *Executive Time Management.* Englewood Cliffs, N.J.: Prentice-Hall, Inc., 1979. Interesting treatment of the importance of proper time distribution in executive work.

CHAPTER TWENTY

Interviews with General Managers

We have talked about the crucial leap into general management for people who wish to vault above a specialty into a broader and higher position. We interviewed three people who have successfully negotiated the leap and asked them how they did it.

Henry Pike testifies:

I was, I feared, a plateaued engineer, and that's the worst kind. I am mechanical in background and joined a large motor car manufacturer right out of engineering school. I started out in the design department, and an interesting aspect was that I came to know how our cars were going to look some years hence.

I worked on a drawing board, developing the specifications for new body design details such as door handles. A designer would come up with a design, and if it passed initial aesthetic approval it was passed on to me to figure out how much it would cost to manufacture the fittings. I would have preferred to do the designing myself, but I am basically a patient man. This was lucky, because I was in this work for three years, with only the most nominal raises.

Someone has said it is no blessing to be born into turbulent times, but I can't agree. About this period our company was undergoing severe competitive pressure from a couple of rivals who were vigorous proponents of heavy innovation based on substantial research and development. We were quite laggard in that regard.

I became a major figure man for the design department. I had made myself quite well acquainted with material costs and labor costs and the director of design implementation came to depend on me as his "abacus man" (or so he called me, out of deference to our Japanese opponents.)

I became something of a threat to the "clay modelers," as we termed the design men whose ideas were eventually transmitted on full-size clay models of automobiles. Many a budding design extravaganza I aborted with my insistence on a rigorous cost study.

On several occasions I was in a meeting room when the all-powerful chairman of the corporation was present. He was a cigar-chompin' bear in his own den.

One day, the C.E.O. was present at a full-dress presentation of the plans for a new sports model being unveiled in our shop. He was there at his intimidating best. One of my bosses was presenting some costs and figures. On one set of them he was way off, for whatever reason. I cleared my throat to say something and then caught myself midway, realizing that I was being insubordinate. The result was a strangled grunt.

The chairman never missed a trick. He heard my grunt of disbelief and, to my consternation, looked straight at me. "You have something to say, young man?" Well, I was trapped, so I said my piece and could feel all the eyes in the room on me.

When my blurt was over, along with the meeting, and I was turning to exit from the room as fast as I could, the chairman put his hand on my shoulder. "What's your name, young man?" he asked, not unkindly. I told him. "You have a good head for figures," he intoned. I thanked him and that seemed that.

The superior whom I had contradicted never said "boo" about the incident. But a few weeks later, when a fine new liaison job between marketing and design opened up, I was in it. It was at the C.E.O.'s insistence.

In this new role, I saw the chairman frequently. Quite often, he relied on me for figures. I must admit that I have a mind like a felt board. Figures stick to it, and thus I almost always had them on my tongue.

A few months later the chairman spoke to me almost casually, saying, "You think you could head our dealer relations office? You'd have to manage a couple of hundred people." I was scared, but game.

The rest of the story: I eventually became vice-president for one of our largest divisions. I'm still someone that the chairman depends on, but as a line manager working on profits and with people, not on disembodied figures.

A second instance of the general management leap happened to a woman named Joan Michaels. She was a college graduate in a recessionary period.

She took a job as a salesperson in women's ready-to-wear in a large department store. She relates her experience:

> Part of the compensation on this job was commission, and month after month I led the section in sales and compensation. I didn't let my achievements go unnoticed, and at several points discussed the possibilities of moving into a supervisory role with the department floor manager.
>
> One day he called me aside and said, "There are no supervisory sales jobs in the works, but how would you like to try the buy side?" I replied that I was sure I could do it, and so was named junior buyer in women's ready-to-wear.
>
> Well, I loved it, and I was good. I seemed to have a gift for sensing fashion, and I had no hesitancy about following my hunches and assessing trends by way of our own sales figures and by shopping other stores.
>
> I found, too, that I got along well with our resources in New York, the manufacturers who made our clothes. I could be tough, which can be hard for a politely-raised woman.
>
> In due course, I became a full-fledged buyer, but I stuck on that rung a long time. This was middle management, but I was ambitious beyond that.
>
> My big break came as a result of a plunge (of necklines, that is). From various bits of information, I developed hunches that necklines were going to plunge, and that shirtwaists or blouses and skirts would be very much in. I went to our resources, and out on a limb, ordering hundreds of low-neckline, simple blouses. I spent several sleepless nights over the order, but I was determined to attract special attention to my prowess.
>
> The neckline worked. We sold out and then some. By the time the quick fad was a couple of weeks old, our competition rendered some similar models. But the fad passed quickly, and they were left holding an inventory full of "dogs," as we say in the trade.
>
> On that one, I got notes of congratulations from the general merchandise manager and the president. I was awarded a nice, fat, extra bonus as well. But best of all, I was brought before one of the board of directors' committees that was investigating our marketing record. This was great visibility.
>
> The general merchandise manager took a particular shine to me in more ways than one. But I was able to stave off his amorous advances and still become the associate merchandise manager of a subsidiary chain, and I'll just bet you that I will be president some day.

Henry Bjorn cannot remember when he didn't want to be a banker. Let him tell his story:

I grew up in a small midwestern city with two banks, and they were the classiest places in town. One had big marble pillars; the other had the most highly varnished wooden floors and check writing tables you've ever seen. The bankers wore white shirts, talked softly, and had courtly manners. They were the most impressive human beings in my world.

I left that world and went to college in the big city, and thence to graduate business school. There was no keeping me "down on the farm" after that.

I joined a big money market bank in the big city and went through what was then a fairly rigorous spate of credit training preparatory to becoming a commercial lending officer with responsibilities for the consumer marketing sector. I stagnated at vice-president for quite a few years and then, at the nervous age of thirty-nine, I got what is commonly known as the big break. I finally got into a species of real management.

What do I mean by that? Well, as you probably know, the average bank lending officer is more of an account executive/salesman than he is a manager. He's in charge of a handful of lending people and a secretary or two, but that's about all. His chances of hopping up into senior command management of the bank are not strong because the pyramid gets so narrow. I was stalled at that narrow neck but good.

I'd had a major soft drink company as my banking client for several years and had worked my way into the confidence of the chief financial officer. He and I sailed together out of the same yacht club but, on the more serious side, I had offered him some damn good advice over the years —if I do say so.

As fate would have it, he was elevated, somewhat to his own surprise, to the post of president and chief operating officer of his company. Shortly thereafter, he called me in and offered me the post of treasurer of his company, with the possible eventuality of becoming chief financial officer. Within eighteen months the financial officer died, and I was moved up.

The president eventually became chairman, and I became president. We're a great team. It's as simple as that.

CHAPTER TWENTY-ONE

Living Styles

For most of his history, it did not occur to the ordinary man that he could live in a style of his own choosing. That luxury was supposedly limited to the rich burghers or the landed aristocrats. With the exception of men who, in all ages, have been rebels and work evaders, the ordinary man considered it his lot in life to toil desperately and steadily in order to meet his obligations. Only in the latter stages of the industrial revolution, with the general push for limitations on working hours and the improvement of working conditions, did people dare to identify the possibility of a decent balance between labor and recreation, family, personal space, or time.

One of the ironies of all this, however, has been that the middle class of people, those who could afford the costs of leisure pursuits, have not had their availability for life's softer pleasures expanded to nearly the extent of the hourly workers they supervise.

The time price of success in the fields we might broadly refer to as managerial has scarcely decreased, despite the fact that official office hours have shrunk. Success is seldom won by hewing to a thirty-eight or forty hour week, particularly in the early and middle stages of a career. The bulging brief cases one sees on the commuter railroads are usually not stage props, but floating offices for people who find too little time to complete their chores during the work day.

There are some exceptions, of course, but a person who places a high premium on lifestyle, which has come to be a synonym for life enjoyment, can find the various demands of management quite a threat.

117

It's cheap and easy and inaccurate to say to a disgruntled, enforced workaholic, "Well, if you don't like it, why don't you quit?" One quickly discovers that the freedom to quit can simply mean the freedom to go jobless, a nearly intolerable state for most of us. How, then, can one civilize work style and improve lifestyle without jeopardizing the job? Various people have come up with various answers.

Jack Myers found that he could enjoy his family more by working at home. He leaves the office regularly at quitting time, seldom goes in to work on weekends, and does a lot of his work at home. Jack is a particularly dedicated family man. He resented those demands of the job that ate into his evenings and weekends and kept him from "growing up with my family," as he put it.

Jack faced a very common dilemma. His work day was filled with people, interviews, phone calls, and "brush fires" to be extinguished. This left little time for the extensive paper work that was expected of him. So, he began to experiment. He carried more and more of his paper work home. He obtained a dictating machine for home and also a good supply of legal pads for writing. He started doing most of his correspondence at home, bringing it to the office for final transcription.

At first he did his home work in his den. While this was cozy, it was a bit remote from the family circle. He began bringing his work into the kitchen, or the living room, or wherever he could be close to the members of his family. At times it required some hard concentration to throw off the natural noises of the kids, but he found himself able to do it. Much of his paper work was relatively routine and thus could be done even in the face of a moderately blaring TV or record player. He could watch his family and be a part of it. He seldom had to tell the kids to pipe down. He was able to get some work done and still enjoy his family.

Likewise, George Kramer found a solution. Simply put, he taught himself to concentrate more and work faster. He found that in the past he had habitually dragged out his work pace, dawdled here, doodled there, passed pleasantries at the water cooler, or prolonged lunches. He would always tell himself that he could stay an extra half-hour or an hour to "clean things up." His extra hours became habitual and of a loose weave similar to that of his regular performance. By changing his habits, by working faster and by running leaner, he was soon able to make it to and from his office on time.

Others have solved part of the time pressure problem by moving in closer to their work places and by adding an hour or two to their work schedules without cutting into their leisure time. Still others turn to working on the commuter train, rather than just sitting, sleeping, reading newspapers, or playing gin rummy.

These have all been devices to correct existing time shortages. How does one guard against such problems at the outset? This is accomplished by knowing demands and by knowing individual organizations and their habits and expectations—these are the principal gauges. Keeping one's eyes always open helps.

Not too long ago I visited an alumnus of our school who is the managing partner of an investment banking firm. There were photographs of three unusually beautiful women in his office. Assuming that these were daughters of whom he would be quite proud, I inquired about these women.

"Oh, those were once my wives," he said. "I loved each of them, but couldn't keep 'em. I am never at home in this work. They wouldn't stand for it."

Investment banking is a known time devourer. So is management consulting. The latter frequently requires a lot of time in airplanes, jetting around the country—and even the world.

Constant travel is a common threat to modern-day managers, particularly in the mid-career years. When a crisis occurs, somebody has to hop on an airplane.

Of course, there are some people who complain about travel but who are really never happier than when they are running for airplanes.

A neighbor of mine was a top-notch management consultant. One day I said to him, "Larry, how does it happen that you seem to travel so seldom when most of your colleagues are never home?"

"It is simple," he replied." I don't enjoy business travel, so I concentrate on getting it over with. When I have a new assignment out of town, I'm careful to plan my trips. I make just a few, but I try to get everything I need on each one. I talk to all the people I need to talk to and I try to pick up all the data I can in one fell swoop. Then, I don't have to go back again very soon. Several of my colleagues are always dashing off to the client's premises, picking up pieces they've forgotten. They waste a great deal of time and money on these trips that would not be really necessary if they were better organized."

As with so many other conditions of employment, the time to determine the lifestyle that the prospective job will require is before you take that job. Too often, in the eagerness to take on a new company or a new assignment, an individual forgets to ask those little questions that later loom so large: How much travel is there? Will I be in control of my time? How work-compulsive are my bosses and my associates? Do they, for example, expect me to work on Saturdays? How long is my vacation? Do people take their allotted vacations or do they tend to work through them? Is overtime encouraged? Have job analyses been performed that will give me some clue as to what will be expected of me?

A fine way to determine the answers to these knotty questions in advance is to talk to peers already with the employer to assess the degree of corporate masochism practiced there.

Anyone who has reached the point of early mid-career recognizes the connection between hard work and success and the fine line between hard work and a neurotic fetish about labor.

The plain fact remains that the majority of the managerial people who succeed in their efforts to amass prestige, power, and money will probably continue to work at least fifty hours a week at one location or another. If it takes these goods to achieve happiness, there is little alternative to one who is dedicated to the profession of management.

Self-Exercise

Time Investment

QUESTION	FILL IN YOUR ANSWERS
Are my hours fair in light of a balance of time for family and recreation?	
Are these hours of my own choosing?	
Do I define my life in terms of both material success and intangible non-work rewards?	

If you answer "no" to the above charted questions, you would be wise to consider adjustments.

CHAPTER TWENTY-TWO

Job Enrichment

It has been said that no person ever carries out a job in the same way his predecessor did. The marks of individuality, creativity, and personal satisfaction are thus revealed.

In these particulars lies the resistance of many managers to think about their successors. Psychologically, they are opposed to the idea that there are people who could adequately fill their roles. The indispensability syndrome is common. It is, therefore, often hard to get a manager to groom a successor, although that is a principal part of the job of any manager.

However, the uses of professional individuality have very powerful benefits.

Work brings multiple satisfactions, not the least of which is the satisfaction derived from doing the best possible job at any assignment. Be it ever so humble, if you can truly say, "I am the best damned (whatever the job is) in the world," you reap a strong reward.

There are at least two sorts of professionals in the world: locals and nationals. A person can be well regarded in his own organization while another, with a similar job, attains national fame in his profession, although this may not be reflected in his status with his employer.

Broad recognition is obtained by figuring prominently in the regional or national affairs of a professional specialty, whether it be a group of certified public accountants, sales managers of a paper box industry, or some

121

general service club such as Lions, Masons, or Kiwanis. Or, it can result from general political activity on any level.

Sometimes called joiners, such people often get more out of and put more into their extracurricular activities than they do their regular jobs.

There's the interesting case of Theodore Grammar. Ted had worked up to a senior underwriter for a casualty insurance company. At age thirty-six, he had progressed from a desk at the front of the open office (or bull pen) to the rear of the office, the more prestigious part, but he was still two doors from the private management offices at the rear of the room. His progress toward management had been a bit less than ordinary for a college graduate. His friend, Harry Davis, on the other hand, who had entered the company the same summer he had, had been ensconced in a private office for two years now.

Ted read the signals clearly. Although he felt secure in the fact that he was a valued employee, he reasoned that he would never rise into higher management. He was valued because of his outstanding technical knowledge. An underwriter in a casualty company passes on the insurance risks his company takes and has a strong hand in setting the rates or premiums paid for the coverage. Ted possessed a quick mathematical mind that earned him the sometime soubriquet of "the human computer."

He had something of the impassive personality of a computer too. An emotionless, flat voice, an almost brusque manner, and a pronounced introvertism were in his nature. He seldom mixed with other people. He ate his lunches solemnly at his desk, chewing on sandwiches and swigging milk as he worked. In appearance, he was small. He was usually garbed in a seedy, shiny suit with lapels of the size that were popular in the previous decade.

Ted was intelligent, and he was aware of his shortcomings that were keeping him from making it into management.

Some of his weaknesses seemed correctable to one of his few friends, Harry Davis, who in the early years endangered that friendship by carping at Ted to improve his ways. Ted proved to be intransigent, preferring to be himself. "You know that's a species of arrogance," Harry reminded him. Ted managed one of his rare and nearly imperceptible smiles, shrugged, and turned back to his "in" file.

Central to Ted's makeup was not arrogance, but pride in his work and his knowledge. Despite his indifference to managerial opportunities, being an expert was very important to him. He loved solving problems that other people found difficult.

Early in his career he had successfully undertaken a rigorous course of study sponsored by the property and casualty insurance industry that led to an award, the designation of Chartered Property and Casualty Underwriter. Ted finished the part-time course with the highest honor. Out of his study he produced a significant paper that proposed a new and broader system for covering the liabilities of ordinary homeowners. It was eagerly published by the main professional journal and was even dubbed the "Grammar Plan," with its advocates called "Grammarians." It was subsequently adopted, with slight alteration, as a new coverage by most of the industry.

Ted did move back one whole desk after this. In addition, he became a regular columnist for the professional journal, advising readers on unusual underwriting problems. He became, in short, a national industry figure. Although he would never make a solo speaker, he was asked to appear on several industry panels as an anchor of reason, if not inspiration.

Ted Grammar had enriched his work life. He had settled for the attainable rather than break his heart over managerial jobs that would not come his way.

Other forms of job enrichment are often dreamed up by the administration of a company to vary the routine existences of workers, supervisors, and executives. Often these experiments take the form of a redivision of a work load and the distribution of the new pieces of work to different people. Such a move avoids routine. It also develops broader people. It may satisfy the human need for change without the necessity of dramatic escalations in status or pay.

Sometimes enrichment takes the form of adding new duties to those that already exist. In this case it is wise to offer some additional pay and to add only duties that are acceptable to the recipient.

Thus, Myron Schoalmaster, an antique fire truck collector, was assigned the additional job of heading his company's volunteer fire department. He was thrilled.

Mary Starbuck, a devoted choral singer, was given the task of organizing a choral group in the same company in addition to her regular job as a quality control supervisor. You'd have thought she had been appointed prima donna at the Metropolitan Opera.

The trick of job enrichment can be for either the employee or his manager to deal with projects and matters that concern them. I recall once appearing before a group of account executives at a major advertising agency. They had been identified as promising "young lions," and the agency was disturbed that they were up to an unusual amount of growling. There was something in their work mix that was not working well.

After several conversations with the group, the picture emerged. Most of them were M.B.A. graduates who were well equipped with scientific management principles and an urge to make use of them. Yet, many felt they were denied this chance. They were assigned to external account work, almost exclusively, acting as go-betweens for the agency and its clients. Often they were reduced to relaying information from one side to the other without initiating any of this information.

What lay at the bottom of this discontent was the fact that the agency itself was poorly run. Its business manager had never had a course in accounting. Its personnel manager was likewise devoid of formal business training. Both were former advertising writers who were unable to make the grade in that specialty.

"What we would like," said a spokesman for the M.B.A. group, "is a chance to roll up our sleeves and clean up the mess inside this company. We don't mean to give up our outside account duties, but to be assigned some additional inside duties."

A young lioness commented further, "This place reminds me of a giant clam. All the musculature is in the shell—outside to repel the clients. Inside it is soft and dark and mushy and contains no pearls."

Before too long, you can surmise, many of these young people were given, in addition to account work, internal assignments. Management of the agency has improved immeasurably. Turnover of disgruntled account people has decreased considerably

Job enrichment has obvious benefits for older employees as well. In some organizations such employees are given a chance to elect somewhat less trying jobs than they have had in the past. This way they can ease into retirement and turn their talents within a company to worthwhile projects they have been itching to complete.

Since we are talking not only about an enriched work life, but an enriched *total* life for early mid-career people, enrichment can come outside the job or in a way that is peripheral to the job. There are ways for any person who will search for work interests and broader interests to lead a fulfilled life. There is not a single person reading this book who is incapable of fostering enthusiasms that will lead to having a better time within or without the main job channel.

It never hurts to push a bit at your place of employment or to make suggestions for change for the better in which you might figure. For you, change for the better means involvement in activities that spark your interest.

Self-Exercise

Enriching Self

QUESTION	FILL IN YOUR ANSWER
Is your current job channel lacking interest and challenge?	

Are there areas at work that contain projects that would interest you that are neglected by your employer?

Do you have talents that can be exploited outside your company on a national, state, or local scale?

Do you possess some special expertise that can be promoted to enhance your fame in a professional sense?

Does your upward advancement seem stymied for reasons that you either cannot or will not control?

"Yes" answers to the questions above are causes to seek job enrichment and life enrichment in order to make your existence more interesting and contributive.

Suggested Readings

BOWER, MARVIN. "Corporate Leaders for the Year 2000." In *Managers for the Year 2000*, edited by William H. Newman, pp. 54–58. Englewood Cliffs, N.J.: Prentice-Hall, Inc., 1978. Agility in coping with change is treated as a managerial necessity.

GARDNER, JOHN W. *Self-Renewal*. New York: Harper & Row, Publishers, Inc., 1963. The definitive work on both personal and organizational self-renewal and enrichment.

LEVINSON, HARRY. *The Great Jackass Fallacy*. Cambridge, Mass.: Harvard University Press, 1973. Delightful treatment of the need for executives to alter their lives and outlooks periodically.

CHAPTER TWENTY-THREE

One's Own Shop

"Someday, I want to have a business of my own." Breathes there a business person who has not at one time or another voiced that sentiment? The small number who will actually assay the act are a special, rare breed. Not that there is a type—just striving individualists with a sense of independence and daring.

First off, as anyone who has attempted the gambit—such as myself—will attest, it requires an almost masochistic strain in a person, because the work hours are endless and the amount of work is enormous. Usually, the person going into business for himself does not want to add to the overhead by hiring the help, expert and otherwise, needed to do the work. As a consequence, the proprietor has to do most of it.

Much of this work is petty, the kinds of things that one happily farms out to others in a bigger organization. There are also some relatively complex tax matters to be handled. Reporting forms to the various governmental levels have to be filled out in the personnel area. There are rent, heat, and electric bills to be paid, as well as contracts to be arranged.

Now and then a group of people break away from a larger entity and start out with a sizeable staff. This is most particularly true in those service businesses where some principals set out with live accounts. Generally speaking, however, new entrepreneurs are founding small enterprises. The biggest things about these firms are their appetites for business. Sometimes this leads to indigestion, due to biting off more than can be rightly chewed.

126

One hears the complaint that too few graduates of the better business schools go into business for themselves. There are several reasons for this.

First off, the schools in question are usually more adept at transmitting attitudes and knowledge for those who will start out in staff work. Then, of course, a start in a new enterprise usually requires some of the kinds of capital that younger people do not have.

There is likewise the lack of in-depth knowledge of a field, any particular field in which the younger person might seek a start. It is my observation that one needs to know a product line, the competition, and some of the people who comprise the market in order to successfully found a new business. There are, of course, always a few exceptions to rules of this sort. Most usually, these are people who have spotted a market opportunity in a brand new field which has hitherto been little exploited in an area. The early laundromat or do-it-yourself picture frame shops are modest retail examples of this sort of activity.

Smaller, self-generated businesses are likely to fail because of inadequate market testing. Is there really a need for the product or service? Typically, the small venturer is so in love with his product or his firm that he fails to believe ill of it—even after market testing has warned him of weaknesses.

In addition to incomplete market testing, faulty bookkeeping and inventory control often assail the amateur businessman. Production can likewise be a problem.

Handling cost allocations is a bugaboo. Generally, these barriers would be less pressing for a business school graduate than for some others.

One of the principal barriers to founding a small business is the matter of raising enough capital to get started. Lending institutions can be obdurate. It takes a sound idea and good salesmanship combined to separate institutional or individual lenders from their money. But it can be done.

A man we know had what was in its time a unique idea. He devised a set of computer programs, or software, that enabled banks to handle with considerable efficacy the management of cash for their corporate customers. The inventor talked to the treasurer of his university who, at that point, was in an unusually venturesome mood. The result was that he invested one million dollars of university funds in the venture. When he recovered from his delight, the young man plowed the largesse into his business with a resultant huge success.

Venture capital firms exist as do venture arms of commercial banks and other financial institutions. If an idea—any idea—is based on sound marketing premise, it will succeed.

Some years ago the father of a student came into the offices of the marketing department of the university where I was then employed. "I have," he proclaimed, "invented a magnificent product. I was hoping that one of your professors could come out and take a look at my setup and advise me on it."

Our chairman was dubious. But, after all, here was a tuition-paying father, and we thought it best to be polite. As the junior member of the faculty, I was assigned to accompany the inventor in question out to his house to see his invention.

The invention was, he said with an air of great secrecy, stored in his garage. It was, he reiterated, a device that would surely revolutionize the life of the housewife and the nation. Shades of Edison!

He opened the door to his garage and a flood of tinkly, shiny, silver metal objects came cascading forth onto the lawn. He excitedly explained that these were unique stainless steel clothespins, the first of their kind—ever. He had his garage stuffed with them, from floor to ceiling.

His points were that these clothespins would never splinter, would hold like iron, and would never rust. I pointed out that clothespins were somewhat on the way out what with electric driers and that the stainless steel version was more expensive than wood or plastic. Tensile they surely were. I could barely get one off my hand. I was grateful it wasn't clamped on my nose.

"These won't do," I said as nicely as I could. "They just won't sell, so I see no reason to perform marketing research." Later, a test was made by some of our students, and the housewives confirmed that plastic and wood clothespins were more suitable and, anyway, electric driers were coming into vogue that rendered any clothespin quite obsolete, just as I had previously told the inventor.

For all I know, that garage full of stainless steel clothespins still stands, a stout monument to product infatuation and market ignorance.

On the other hand, here are two monuments to successful small businesses that got off the ground beautifully. Some years ago, Miles Kirk was a salesman for a huge computer manufacturer. He specialized in the sale of the punched cards that were a vital part of computer operations in those days. He was most successful at his charge, establishing a rich and deep clientele in his home city. Gradually, it occurred to Miles that he virtually controlled a substantial market. It likewise occurred to him that he could manufacture a better card and sell it for less. He tied in with a production foreman from his current employer. The two of them opened their own shop. They were able to switch about half of the current customers over to their new firm and its product. Today their concern has 1,000 employees and is a substantial factor in the manufacture and marketing of various peripheral devices for the computer.

Similar prior control of a market was characteristic of the foundation of a substantial advertising agency that has prospered over the years. Aristide Brion also originated as a salesman. He sold advertising space for a fleet of insurance trade magazines.

His clientele consisted of smaller advertisers of a type that did not in that day use advertising agencies. Instead, the clients relied on the magazines to devise their advertising — to write it, to design it, and to set it up in type and illustrations. If he wanted to sell an ad, Aristide had to draw it up and execute it. He became remarkably adept at the job and built up a clientele of some twenty-six advertisers who depended on him for their ads. In short, he was performing an advertising agency service for his clients and receiving for his pains only his commission and salary from the magazines.

Aristide took the obvious step for a man of enterprise. He proposed to his clients that he act as their ad agency. Most of them accepted. Hiring an agency of known quality cost them nothing extra because the medium (the magazines) followed the custom of their trade to pay the ad agency 15 percent of the space cost. Aristide quit the magazine, kept most of the accounts, and was in business. Voila!

A factor mitigating against more entries of well-educated people into their own enterprises is a species of social caste. Well-bred and educated young people will not sleep in the backs of stores and work at rough jobs to get the enterprises going the way their fathers and grandfathers did. As a consequence, many smaller and retail-oriented opportunities go begging as far as college people are concerned. Running gas stations, laundromats, hamburger stands, and various kinds of motel, service, and retail establishments have been considered beyond the respectable pale.

This also extends to the various franchise opportunities open to prospective owners-managers. Many fast-food restaurants are operated on this basis.

I know a man who was for many years in the advertising agency business as an art director and an account executive. He worked on a fast-food account in the agency. Gradually, he was drawn to the idea of switching himself into a franchised hamburger store in a more pleasant climate. Finally, he quit the agency and went through with his plan.

In the first few months he wondered what kind of a bargain he had made with the devil. He had a hard time finding an adequate staff for his business and then paying for that staff when he found it. He, his wife, and his children worked the counter, the stove, and the dishwasher. They worked their elegant upper middle class fingers to the bone.

Gradually, they built a staff and earned plenty to pay them. They bought franchises at a couple of other stations and they have prospered as well. The man in question has put his promotional experience to work by inventing a new kind of meal that has been adopted for the whole chain.

On the whole, small business appears to have been losing rather than gaining ground in the United States. This may remove what up until now has been a major source of innovation, expansion, and creativity. Although small business still accounts for something like three out of four of all private sector jobs, there is evidence that its relative role is shrinking. The failure rate has had a way of exceeding the start-up rate since 1974, the opposite of the experience of larger businesses.

Part of the unfavorable story is that inflation apparently falls with more severity on small business. Then, too, small business operates with higher ratios of debt. Insufficient cash flow is classic.

Despite these troubles, there continue to be new businesses aggressively seeking out new opportunities while many larger ones are primarily redistributing their operations.

Self-Exercise

Geared to Your Own Business

QUESTION	FILL IN YOUR ANSWER
Do you have the courage to try, knowing that the bulk of small businesses die quickly after birth?	
Do you have an appetite for grueling work and long hours?	
Can you put up with handling a multiplicity of petty details?	
Do you have a keen nose for the market?	
Do you understand accounting?	
Would you prefer the profitable to the fashionable?	
Do you know a particular set of products well?	
Do you know a market well? Do you know some customers or potential customers in that market? Do you have access to that market?	
Are you able to make crisp decisions on your own without the protective paraphernalia of a committee?	

If you have affirmations for all the above, plus robust health, energy, and a burning desire for independence and some capital, you can consider hanging out your shingle.

Suggested Reading

BROOM, H. N., and LONGNECKER, T. E. *Small Business Management.* 5th ed. Cincinnati, Ohio: South-Western Publishing Co., 1979. Classic advice for embarkers on small business ventures.

CHAPTER TWENTY-FOUR

The Shifting Grail

The shifting nature of the human personality, the changes in desires, aims, and goals, render humans fascinating, although at times very frustrated, creatures.

We've all had the experience of wanting something intensely at one point and, having achieved it, finding that it isn't what we really wanted after all. Does this mean that we are will-o'-the-wisps, ephemeral persons with no stability? Far from it. It is testimony that man is a learning creature who profits by growth, mistakes, and discoveries. The human being, as has been observed in earlier chapters, is subject to various physiological and psychological changes at various stages in life. In addition to these more or less predictable changes, all sorts of individual idiosyncrasies arise.

If you foisted the same lecture notes on a class year after year, the students would know it, and you would feel out of date. Every lecturer worth his or her salt changes from year to year in his or her aims and perceptions. Read a letter that you wrote a few years back. Would you write the same today?

Dr. Milne was near the top of his profession. A renowned surgical professor, he was lionized by his colleagues and by the public. He was happy until a friend of his showed him Shangri-La. Shangri-La was a beautiful resort in every way but in its nonsubtle name. It was on an Ozark mountain lake. It was for sale to the highest bidder.

Dr. Milne lusted to buy it, to run it, to convert it into a health sanitorium and spa, and to live in it. He spent his waking hours thinking about it, cutting down on his surgical practice and his teaching, spending his weekends on the scene, scarring his surgical hands with dirt and fish hooks. Finally, he bought it and became the proprietor of a reasonably successful sanitorium. One had a hunch he'd even do it for pleasure, with far less profit. Medicine continued to interest him, but in a more generalized way.

Changes in career aims are not necessarily pronounced—at least not prior to retirement. Oh, there are whims and urges people have to throw the past out all together—to open chicken farms instead of running advertising agencies or to become shrimp boat captains instead of stockbrokers. These sorts of things, which one might characterize as "back to the land" philosophy, will always tend to have some appeal and also their share of failures. It's the other side of the coin of appeal that has drawn millions away from the farms over the last 100 years. However, by and large, such moves to cities and towns were carried on by people who were not very professionally career committed. They had no great professional stakes in the process. The moves were induced by massive peer pressures coupled with economic necessity.

There is nothing wrong with drastically different or distinct shifts in operation. It's just that they seldom work. When a person strays, at a fairly late stage in life, too far from what he or she has been trained to do, he or she will have a tough time making a go of it, although one can cite examples of such success. This does not necessarily apply to the work-play aspect of the retired person, but this is, after all, a book written for persons who can scarcely plan retirement yet—people who are not removed from the necessity of making a fair living.

What we are talking about here are those changes in aims and direction that propel people toward reasonably revised occupational goals.

As one ambitious man put it, "Just before I go to sleep at night, I think of a glass door. On this door is painted my name, with the shiny new title 'vice-president.' Usually, I am able to go to sleep smiling."

We're talking about something of a somewhat longer range than "vice-president" on the door, but there is nothing wrong with such a goal. We're talking about a dream, if you will, of what will bring work satisfaction and lifestyle satisfaction to the dreamer.

And why shouldn't work pursuits be just as important as this vaunted thing everybody now calls lifestyle? They aren't quite the same, but they meld into making a life worth living. Oh, there are a few in this world who enjoy a lifestyle of doing nothing, and many more who think they would. Some sun themselves on the left side in the A.M. and on the right side in the P.M., with a fancy lunch in between. We may all suspect that we'd like such a lifestyle, but listen to Helen:

What was I? I was a rich bitch, like a pet chameleon. Remember those little lizards on a string that our Dads used to buy us at the circus? Except they changed color. I was more like a leopard on a chain. I picked up spots from the sun. I got too much of it. Made me look kind of old, and I'm only thirty-five.

I had nothing to do. My husband, Harry, worked all day, but he did take me out some at night when he was in town. Big deal! I read a lot—some pretty good books. But books aren't life. Sometimes I picked up a bit of sex from the beach boys. Mostly they're animals who act like I am an old washing machine or something. They don't pant like Harry, or pat me affectionately on the behind like he does, or tell me I'm still okay and sorta' mean it.

Listen, with all this dough, I got fed up. I decided to get a job. I had a nice car, and I knew the hotels on that beach backward and forward. I had connections, too. So I started out being a convention salesperson for the Ardmore Hotel, selling to those in the northern cities. Harry was a little dubious, but he's a dear. He says he misses me when I travel, and that's nice to know. You know, for the first time, I'm living.

You've just got in on the start of the career of one of America's most successful convention hotel arrangers. It was not just the start of a career; it was the start of a happy blend of living elements.

For most people, an idyllic lifestyle is not enough. Most of us need to be doing something to win our own approval and the approval of the society in which we live.

It is hard to achieve this ideal before early mid-career. If we wait too long, however, it can be too late.

The shifts we are talking about will, in all probability, come about as alternatives to the dream at the start of the career. Usually, that dream had some substance—unlike the ephemeral word "dreams" in the usual nightly meaning. There was a deep, emotional, character-related hunger to the dream that made a sanitorium keeper out of a physician and a convention booker out of a wealthy wife. Either one of them could have probably quit and done nothing, even though they were still at middle life. But both had an urge to serve, to be generative, and to use some of the things they felt they had learned from life to help other people.

They changed and they succeeded, but they stayed true to what was basically their original dream.

Now, everyone need not necessarily be generative, but the point of this book is not to suggest that you wait until retirement to reach a balance, a fruition, and a contentment. Whatever form of satisfaction one seeks, it is attainable at least by the time one gets the feet a little wet.

Self-Exercise

Something Else, Within Reason

QUESTION	FILL IN YOUR ANSWER
Is there an occupation you might like to switch to within the near future?	
Are you equipped with skills for it?	
Could you get a job at it or finance it?	
Have you talked to people who have done it?	
Does it really make your blood race?	

If you say "yes" to these questions, start investigating.

Suggested Readings

Livesey, Herbert B. *Second Chance–Blueprints for Life Change.* Philadelphia, Pa.: J. B. Lippincott Company, 1977.

Pearse, Robert F., and Peltzer, B. Purdy. *Self-Directed Change in the Mid-Career Manager.* New York: AMACOM, 1975.

Robbins, Paula I. *Successful Mid-Life Career Change.* New York: AMACOM, 1978.

CHAPTER TWENTY-FIVE

Tactics for Recession

As we all know, despite the fulminations of economists and other experts, we face many ups and downs on the economic charts. Clearly, any attempts at forecasting are feeble exercises at best. A career is like a marriage. The vows are taken for richer or for poorer, and during the poorer periods strains on the relationship can be stronger.

Clearly, a stronger economy means a stronger career market in general. However, the canny career planner can cope with adversity and even put it to his use.

The plain truth is, as any executive search consultant will attest, that there is a perpetual shortage of executive talent—and there always will be. Emphasis here is on the word "talent," that combination of personal traits, knowledge, and experience that makes men and women valuable to their organizations, to their associates, and to themselves.

Many a lukewarm manager can limp along in the best of times. The uses of adversity are such that it is in the most cruel of times that he runs the danger of becoming dispensable. And it is in the rough periods that the challenges lie for those who want to work themselves up to being valuable. Such a working up calls for brains, motivation, and industry. Happily for the many successful people who are not Mensa material—that is, those who are not at the apex of raw cerebral power—hard work and harnessed motivation are even stronger allies than brains. It is the harnessing, the deliberate planning, that can make the difference. Less favorable times often provide their own uses for such people.

There is the case of General Eisenhower, no mental giant by his own admission. He languished for nine long years as a modest major until impending war provided him the opportunity to become the highest military officer in the Allied cause in World War II.

The analogy of war and recession is not far-fetched. There is a military parallel to business. We speak of business "campaigns." Sales forces are the "front line troops." We "bombard" consumers with advertising. Our "line and staff" distinctions are military derivatives. When campaigning is tough, business managers get a better chance to show their mettle and to win their medals.

Take, for example, David Ardsleigh. For some years he was a branch manager for a large, British manufacturer of small ticket household goods. Britain's local markets were plagued with recession, layoffs, and attendant unemployment. The bottom had fallen out of the domestic market.

David cast about in his own mind and in his own company. Where in the world could opportunities lie to bolster sales? He contrasted the plight of petrol-starved Britain with the oil-based economic fortunes of Saudi Arabia.

David first picked up a library acquaintance with Saudi Arabia. Then he made the acquaintance of the several people within his company who possessed Near Eastern and Middle Eastern experience. These people largely constituted those who had been "out there" in India, Pakistan, Egypt, and Lebanon, where his company had markets that had over the years "followed the flag" but that in recent years had set up national barriers to British goods.

He attended some local college course offerings in the Arabic languages and Islamic culture. One of his teachers was a Saudi gentleman who arranged for him to spend an arid but fruitful holiday in the Saudi capital. He also provided introductions for him to some of the principal consumer goods distributors in his country.

In the meantime, David had secured, from the export manager of his company, permission to explore the opening of trade relations with the Saudis. This he did with several influential distributors. He came back with an agreement with one agent, who was in good stead with the ruling Saudi regime, to distribute several household and proprietary products in that country.

The market flourished, and so did David. He subsequently became export manager for the Middle East and turned his talents to other nations of the Arab world as well.

There are numerous instances of eager young managers with sharp pencils bringing about financial and operational savings in a corporation that are so crucial in harder times.

Sheila Montgomery was a cost accountant, by training and by inclination, with a grain factoring company in Minneapolis. It was the custom of that company to load grain from various midwestern ports on the Mississippi to go down river to gulf ports for export. They were forced to pay increasingly steep fees to the barge-owning companies for these shipments.

Privately, Sheila got in touch with a barge building and refurbishing facility near St. Paul that was headed by a university classmate of hers. He agreed to explore the possibility of lease/buy arrangements through which Sheila's firm could lease, with option to buy, some second-hand, renovated grain barges.

Sheila transmitted this possibility to the head of her company, who was quite delighted when shown that such an exchange could make a difference of $2,000 a load in shipping arrangements and eventually lead to ownership of a small fleet of barges. This option was subsequently enlarged to include a few tow boats, at further savings.

Sheila had integrated the distribution of grain into the total operations of her company and had integrated herself into the position of controller. Eventually, she transferred her talents to the more important job of vice-president and director of transportation in another larger company.

Inflation, recession, and similar adversities thus can add to the opportunities to prove useful and to shine for those who work at ways of improving the cost or market position of a company that is being squeezed. Heightened opportunities abound for those who will apply ingenuity in the face of external exigencies.

It is in such times that companies can least afford to hire expensive outside consulting counsel to help them with their mounting problems. Every alert and trained insider thus has a chance to provide this counsel. It takes extra effort—extra pain—to serve in this role, but it can be well worth both.

Self-Exercise

Recession Tactics

1. What are the economic pressure points most trying to our organization?

2. What can I devise to ease that pressure in the operations area, the finance area, or the marketing area?

3. How do I gain the information necessary to devise new strategy?

4. How can I proceed to implement that strategy?

5. How can I market my achievement in a way that will advance me up the career ladder?

CHAPTER TWENTY-SIX

Job Hunting in a Nutshell

Many writers of books on job hunting have been less interested in their readers than in creating income for themselves. Quite a few such writers are not particularly or peculiarly equipped for the task because they know of most jobs on a second-hand basis. They are about as well suited, experientially, as a celibate priest is to talk about the variety of experiences in the sexual act. Yet, they persist, and sell tomes on how to write résumés, how to prospect, how to advertise, and how to interview. They feed on the apparently bottomless appetite of the vast audience of the itchy-footed or those who find themselves between jobs.

Whatever the causes for a job search, reading the reams of books is basically repetitive. They all boil down to the following strictures:

1. Decide what you want and where you want it (that is, the job and the employer).

2. Study the company to find out more about it.

3. Talk to the people at the company who make the real hiring decisions in your area of interest. They may be operating people. At any rate, you need to know their names. You may find some of the right names from *Moody's*, the *College Placement Annual,* and various other directories to be found in libraries and in the annual reports of companies. The danger is that people who *appear* to have hiring authority often have little of it.

4. Through acquaintances, try to arrange meetings with the appropriate people.

5. Letters of introduction, written by applicants or friends, to key people—with or without résumés—make sense. Unfocused mass mailings are desperation measures. Write only as many letters as you can follow up with phone calls fairly soon after mailing them.

6. Executive search firms can be useful to relatively highly placed people, usually over thirty years of age. Selected mailings to these firms can make sense. A national list can be obtained from American Management Association, with offices in the major cities. Executives of some search firms are sometimes willing to suggest other search firms that they honor. Check with friends and acquaintances as to the firms they have found helpful.

There is some argument over whether a résumé should or should not be sent with prospecting letters. For those with strong résumés and records, we feel that a résumé (or curriculum vitae, as it is often called) can do no harm. If the summary presents gaps or discrepancies, a carefully written letter can often cover some of the tracks better than a résumé.

7. Firms that help individual job seekers may bolster the unsure, but be wary. They will charge substantial fees for helping with résumé writing, for circulating the résumé, and for psychological testing. Beware, particularly, of the testing or psychological gambit. Most career people have a fair idea of what they are fit for—if they will think it out for themselves. As we have indicated elsewhere, this is a key and salutary exercise.

If you feel you are having some psychological problems, seek out a good industrial psychologist—one who knows about business careers. The personnel officers of most major companies can provide some leads to reputable practitioners.

8. It is well to avoid employment agencies as such. They are, at best, courts of last resort for managerial people. The jobs they come across are usually at low levels. Executive employers view the reputations of the best of them as hard-selling body merchants who cast a shadow over the applicants who are sent out from them.

9. For job seekers but a few years out of the university, the alumni placement office can be a good reference point. This is particularly true of those connected with schools of business, although the degree of helpfulness even of these varies all over. Services of alumni placement offices can include ample libraries, company annual reports, and files; live job openings sent in by industry and nonprofit employers; help with résumés; and, in some cases, circulation of résumés to prospective employers. They are not, however, likely to have registered with them general management jobs or staff jobs in the higher sense.

10. Newspaper and magazine advertisements can be a source of leads, the so-called "want ads." Major daily newspapers, business newspapers, and trade and professional journals are the most fruitful sources. The latter abound, for in most functional managerial fields there is a journal or two of some repute.

On a similar score, professional associations and their meetings can be fruitful sources for those who have paid literal and figurative dues to them over the years.

Occasionally an applicant will place his or her own advertisements in periodicals of one sort or another. This is done especially when the applicant has some particularly arresting experiences or skills to sell.

The yield from either reading or placing advertisements is low, but it is like fishing. Some very big catches can be made, and the route should not be ignored.

11. It can be very discouraging to launch a job search during the summer. Prospective employers are either not in or are in no mood to add employees. The Christmas season is a low period also, since employers are preoccupied with the holidays. Generally, the other months of fall, winter, and spring are quite suitable.

12. Landing a good new job that represents advancement over the current one takes time. Six months is not out of the question. However, one may, of course, hit in the first week or two.

Care must be taken not to grab the first thing that comes along out of frustration with the process. This is true even for the person out of work. He or she may be letting himself or herself in for the same sort of frustration that drove him or her from the previous job.

13. One leads from greater strength if he or she is currently holding a good job. But there are trade-offs. Usually, when one is searching for a new job while fully employed, he or she has security worries. Will he or she be found out and thus be weakened or sacked? Also, the employed seeker has a number of limitations upon his or her time. Job hunting is indeed an extra job that requires substantial time.

14. One should try to keep up the flavor of resignation even in those cases in which he or she has actually been forced out. Most former employers are willing to cooperate on this score. Of course, this and subsequent recommendations must be watched by hirers. The mid-career person faced with hiring decisions must take that into account.

There are all kinds of ameliorating circumstances surrounding layoffs or firings. Certain companies are well known to be in economic stagnation or recession. Others have been merged or taken over, forcing managers out into the streets. Future employers will easily forgive such reasons for dismissal.

Certain enlightened employers will, in the case of their terminated employees, proffer them the service of executive search consultants who are strictly in the business of "out-placement." These services are optional —at no cost to the recipient—and such counsel has been known to be of great help to those who have gotten the gate.

15. The applicant should not lead with a discussion of money terms, but, of course, remuneration is of importance. Let the employer initiate the salary discussion. When finally cornered as to price, quote a range rather than a solid figure.

Negotiate, negotiate! That is at the heart of business. Never be embarrassed to ask for more. Expect some display of discomfiture from the employer when you ask, but that is a part of the game.

The best way to ask for more money is to say, "Mr. Smedley, I am impressed with you and your organization. I am intrigued with the challenge. There is one other small point about which I would like to inquire. Could the salary please be reexamined, since it falls somewhat below my needs and expectations?"

Usually, the matter can indeed be reexamined. Far from truly annoying most employers, it will increase the respect the employer has for the applicant.

The point at which to ask for the maximum goodies is the hiring point. It is also the time to press for an improved title and other perquisites such as moving (and perhaps housing) arrangements. Catch the employer while he or she lusts for you, or perhaps you will later find yourself in a far less seductive position.

How much more money should you ask for on the new job? If you're leading from the strength of being sought, at least 25 percent makes good sense. If you are in more of a supplicant's position, 25 percent may be a bit strong.

Remember that the cost of breaking ties, of interrupting a pension, and (in some cases) of seriously disrupting family life is high.

Remember, too, your own chartings. Make sure, if possible, that the new post represents not only a raise in pay but a growth in responsibility as well.

In short, sic 'em!

Suggested Readings

BOLL, CARL R. *Executive Jobs Unlimited.* New York: Macmillan, Inc., 1965. Excellent advice for the executive seeking a new job.

BOLLES, RICHARD N. *What Color Is Your Parachute?* Berkeley, Ca.: Ten Speed Press, 1976. Probably the most widely read text on job hunting, and rightly so.

BOROS, JAMES M., and PARKINSON, T. ROBERT. *How to Get a Fast Start in Today's Job Market.* Englewood Cliffs, N.J.: Prentice-Hall, Inc., 1980. Although written essentially for students, this book contains pointers across the board that are helpful to job searchers of any age.

CRYSTAL, JOHN C., and BOLLES, RICHARD N. *Where Do I Go from Here with My Life?* New York: Seaburg Press, 1974. A detailed plan for building and expanding a network of personal contacts through the use of systematic targeting.

FIGLER, HOWARD. *The Complete Job Search Handbook.* New York: Holt, Rinehart & Winston, 1979. Thorough and interesting summary of job-hunting techniques by an outstanding placement director.

JACKSON, TOM, and MAYLEAS, DAVIDYNE. *The Hidden Job Market.* New York: Quadrangle The New York Times Book Co., 1976. Explains how the simplest forms of job market research involve combing numerous publications that are widely available.

JEFFERS, WILLIAM. *Selling Yourself: The Way to a Better Job.* Englewood Cliffs, N.J.: Prentice-Hall, Inc., 1979. Treats job hunting as the total marketing project that it is.

LUKOWSKI, SUSAN, and PITON, MARGARET. *Strategy and Tactics for Getting a Government Job.* Washington, D.C.: Potomac Books, 1972. Some dated information, but a good framework for the sector.

Appendix:
Reference Sources

Bibliographies

DANIELLS, LORNA M., *Business Information Sources.* Berkeley: University of California—A standard annotated guide to business reference sources and basic texts.

WASSERMAN, PAUL, *Encyclopedia of Business Information Sources.* (4th ed.) Detroit: Gale Research, 1980—A more comprehensive and current work than Daniells' work, but lacks annotations. Includes general as well as extremely specialized trade reference sources.

General Information

Standard & Poor's Industry Surveys—Gives overviews of selected industries, including basic statistics and financial comparisons of the major companies within each.

Value Line Investment Survey—Also gives overviews of selected industries and major companies within each, although the emphasis here is on information concerning stocks.

Directories of Companies

Dun & Bradstreet, Inc., *Million Dollar Directory*—In two volumes. Vol. I covers companies with assets greater than $1 million and Vol. II covers companies worth $500,000 to $999,999. Basic entries include a listing of officers and directors, annual sales, products, and a number of employees. Indexes list companies by geographical area and product classification.

Standard & Poor's Register of Corporations, Directors, and Executives —Covers major U.S. and international companies. Basic entries are similar to those in D & B *Directory* and, likewise, indexes list companies by geographical area and product classification. A separate volume provides biographical information on selected directors and executives.

Detailed Information

Moody's *Manual* series (includes *Bank and Finance Manual, Industrial Manual, Municipal and Government Manual, OTC Industrial Manual, Public Utility Manual,* and *Transportation Manual*)—Covers U.S. and foreign companies listed on American exchanges. Includes a brief corporate history, a list of subsidiaries, officers and directors, balance sheet statistics, and descriptions of outstanding securities. Information is updated weekly or biweekly.

Standard & Poor's *Corporation Records*—Similar in nature to Moody's. Daily news section is updated every business day and conveniently indexed.

Corporate 10-K and Annual Reports. Many libraries receive current 10-K and annual reports of NYSE, AMEX, and OTC companies on microfiche.

Periodicals Indexes Covering Articles About Companies

    I. General
        Business Periodicals Index
        F & S Index of Corporations and Industries
    II. Single-title
        Wall Street Journal Index
        New York Times Index
        Chicago Tribune Index
    III. Specialized
        Accountant's Index
        Insurance Periodicals Index

Index